Computer Simulations
of Voting Behavior

STUDIES IN BEHAVIORAL POLITICAL SCIENCE

Series editor Robert Presthus

Also in the series:

POLITICAL SOCIALIZATION, *Kenneth P. Langton*

Other volumes in preparation:

POLITICAL VALUES OF AMERICAN PHYSICAL
  SCIENTISTS, *Vaughn Blankenship*
CONSEQUENCES OF INFLUENCE IN INTERNA-
  TIONAL POLITICS, *Raymond Tantor*
THE JUDICIAL MIND RE-VISITED, *Glendon Schubert*

Computer Simulations of Voting Behavior

WILLIAM R. SHAFFER

Purdue University

New York
OXFORD UNIVERSITY PRESS
London   1972   Toronto

To my parents
THOMAS R. *and* MARIAN E. SHAFFER

PREFACE

Any effort to produce a scholarly work cannot be successfully undertaken without the assistance provided by one's colleagues and associates. Needless to say, all of those who have contributed to this writer's research are too numerous to mention.

Nevertheless, special thanks is gratefully extended to Frank Munger for his thoughtful and imaginative suggestions during the research and writing stages of the present study. In addition, Wayne Francis deserves acknowledgment for the intellectual stimulation which prompted the author's fascination with scholarly empirical research. The author is also grateful for the thoughtful suggestions and personal friendship of Ronald E. Weber, who has been most helpful throughout this writer's professional career. Furthermore, the editorial advice of Robert Presthus was an invaluable asset in revising the earlier manuscript. Moreover, further refinement of the book would not have been accomplished without the editorial assistance of James Amon and Deborah Zwecher.

Also, the author wishes to thank Kay McKenny for typing the original manuscript with both skill and patience. Revisions were competently typed by Dorothy Eberle, Janet Hasser, Mary Wilkinson, and Jeanne Williams.

The Syracuse University Computer Center should be mentioned for the use of its computer facilities. The tables and charts in Chapters 4, 5, and 6 are the author's but the data were made available by the Inter-University Consortium for Political Research. The data were originally collected by the Michigan Survey Research Center. Neither the SRC nor the

Consortium bear any responsibility for the analyses or interpretations presented here.

Finally, I am grateful to my wife, Pat, for her patience, love, and understanding. Her encouragement was a source of strength which is so necessary for an undertaking of this sort.

W.R.S.

Lafayette, Indiana
January 1972

CONTENTS

LIST OF TABLES   *viii*
LIST OF FIGURES   *xii*

1   Introduction   *3*
2   Computer Simulation as a Research Technique   *10*
3   Models of Voter Decision-Making   *19*
4   Measuring Downsian Model Parameters   *69*
5   Downsian Model Simulation Results   *80*
6   SRC Six-Component Simulation Results   *119*
7   A Revised Process Model of Voting Behavior   *137*

APPENDICES
A   Survey Items Included in Factor Analysis   *148*
B   Summary of Results for Sensitivity Tests
        of Downsian Models   *153*

BIBLIOGRAPHY   *154*
INDEX   *160*

LIST OF TABLES

TABLE

4.1 Rotated Factor Loadings—1964 Survey Items *74–75*

5.1 Summary Statistics for Original Model, All Parameters at Full and Equal Weight *81*

5.2 Original Model, Simulation and Actual Results for Those with Non-Zero Party Differentials *83*

5.3 Original Model, Simulation and Actual Results for Those with Zero Party Differentials (Perceive Different Policies, Same Utility) *84*

5.4 Original Model, Simulation and Actual Results for Those with Zero Party Differentials (Perceive Same Policies) *86*

5.5 Summary Statistics for Cost Experiment with Parameter Weight Equal to 0.0 *91*

5.6 Information Cost Experiment, Simulation and Actual Results for Those with Non-Zero Party Differentials, Parameter Weight Equal to 0.0 *92*

5.7 Information Cost Experiment, Simulation and Actual Results for Those with Zero Party Differentials (Perceive Different Policies, Same Utility), Parameter Weight Equal to 0.0 *93*

5.8 Information Cost Experiment, Simulation and Actual Results for Those with Zero Party Differentials

TABLE

(Perceive Same Policies), Parameter Weight Equal to 0.0   *95*

5.9   Summary Statistics for Perceived Closeness of Election Experiment with Parameter Weight Equal to 0.0   *96*

5.10   Perceived Closeness of Election Experiment, Simulation and Actual Results for Those with Non-Zero Party Differentials, Parameter Weight Equal to 0.0   *97*

5.11   Summary Statistics for Long-Run Participation Value Experiment with Parameter Weight Equal to 0.0   *98*

5.12   Long-Run Participation Value Experiment, Simulation and Actual Results for Those with Non-Zero Party Differentials, Parameter Weight Equal to 0.0   *99*

5.13   Summary Statistics for Party Identification Modification of Original Model with All Parameters at Full and Equal Weight   *101*

5.14   Party Identification Modification of Original Model, Simulation and Actual Results for Those with Zero Party Differentials and Non-Zero Party Identification   *103*

5.15   Party Identification Modification of Original Model, Simulation and Actual Results for Those with Zero Party Differentials (Perceive Different Policies, Same Utility)   *104*

5.16   Party Identification Modification of Original Model, Simulation and Actual Results for Those with Zero Party Differentials (Perceive Same Policies)   *105*

5.17   Summary Statistics for Party Identification, Cost Parameter Weight Equal to 0.0   *107*

TABLE

5.18   Party Identification Modification—Cost Experiment, Simulation and Actual Results for Those with Non-Zero Party Identifications   *109*

5.19   Party Identification Modification—Cost Experiment, Simulation and Actual Results for Those with Non-Zero Party Differentials (Perceive Same Policies)   *110*

5.20   Summary Statistics for Ideological Modification with All Parameters at Full Weight   *111*

5.21   Ideological Modification, Simulation and Actual Results for Those with Non-Zero Ideological Differentials   *113*

5.22   Summary Statistics for Ideological Modification, Cost Parameter Weight Equal to 0.0   *116*

5.23   Ideological Modification—Cost Experiment, Simulation and Actual Results for Those with Non-Zero Ideological Differentials   *117*

6.1   SRC Six-Component Model, Simulation and Actual Results   *120*

6.2   Original SRC Six-Component Model, Simulation and Actual Results   *121*

6.3   Per Cent Correctly Predicted by Parameter for Each of the SRC Six Components   *123*

6.4   SRC Six-Component Model Democratic Candidate Perceptions Experiment, Simulation and Actual Results, Parameter Weight Equal to 0.0   *125*

6.5   SRC Six-Component Model Republican Candidate Perceptions Experiment, Simulation and Actual Results, Parameter Weight Equal to 0.0   *127*

6.6   SRC Six-Component Model Group-Related Response Parameter Weight Equal to 0.0   *128*

6.7   SRC Six-Component Model Domestic Issues Percep-

TABLE

tions Experiment, Simulated and Actual Results, Parameter Weight Equal to 0.0   *130*

6.8   SRC Six-Component Model Foreign Policy Perceptions
Experiment, Simulation and Actual Results,
Parameter Weight Equal to 0.0   *131*

6.9   SRC Six-Component Model Government Management
Perceptions Experiment, Simulation and Actual
Results, Parameter Weight Equal to 0.0   *134*

6.10   Unrotated Factor Loadings for SRC Six-Component
Scores—1964 Presidential Election   *135*

6.11   Distribution of Respondents by Partisan Direction on
Each Component (in Per Cent)   *136*

LIST OF FIGURES

FIGURE

1.1   Theoretical Levels of Analysis   *5*

2.1   "Predisposition Phase" of Shapiro's Roll-Call Voting
      Model   *13*

2.2   "Linkage" Phase of Shapiro's Roll-Call Voting
      Model   *14*

3.1   Cross-Pressure Pattern   *23*

3.2   Flow Diagram of McPhee's Socio-Psychological
      Model   *34*

3.3   Stimulus Intensity Table Stored in Computer   *38*

3.4   Flow Diagram of Two People Going Through
      McPhee's Socio-Psychological Model   *42*

3.5   Flow Diagram of Downsian Decision-Making
      Model   *62–63*

3.6   Flow Diagram of Survey Research Center
      Six-Component Model   *68*

5.1   Summary of Parameter Experiments Original
      Model   *89*

5.2   Summary of Parameter Experiments Party Identifica-
      tion Modification   *106*

5.3   Summary of Parameter Experiments Ideological
      Modification   *115*

7.1   Revised Voting Process Model   *144–45*

Computer Simulations
of Voting Behavior

1 Introduction

This is a study of the voter's decision-making process. Its major focus is on the acts, cognitions, and emotions which, when combined, constitute a coherent series of events leading to the voting decision. The author will be concerned with various models designed to offer accounts of the process by which voters select the candidate of their choice.

This research differs from the usual approach to the analysis of electoral behavior. In the past the general format for voting analysis has been to state some hypotheses which were amenable to empirical analysis. Subsequent testing of these hypotheses facilitated a discussion of reputedly relevant parameters of voting behavior. The sophistication of the methodology employed has ranged from simple frequency counts and cross-tabulations to correlation and regression analysis.

Through the usual process, many extremely important findings have been produced for the particular elections analyzed. Generalizations for all elections can be made from many of these results. For example, consider the proposition that the degree to which an individual identifies with a given party is a basic part of his political outlook. This concept of partisan attachment has received virtually universal recognition as a major determinant of voting behavior.[1] No other independent variable appears to have the impact that party identification has on par-

[1] For example, see Angus Campbell, Philip E. Converse, Warren E. Miller, and Donald E. Stokes, *The American Voter* (New York: John

tisan choice. Furthermore, the empirical evidence not only confirms the impact of party loyalty on the electoral decision, but also demonstrates that partisan attachment affects the perception of the policy stands of parties and candidates.[2]

Other important findings concerning such factors as social class, primary group behavior, psychological involvement, sense of citizen duty, ideology, policy, etc., have similarly expanded our knowledge and understanding of the realities of voting behavior.

The general methodological approach of this book will be to examine the voting act as a *process*. Rather than look at a limited number of statistical relationships, we will be concerned with testing voter decision-making models. The application of various models will facilitate an analysis of the elections brought under consideration.

The models of voting behavior used here can be classified into three theoretical levels of analysis: sociological, socio-psychological, and psychological.

Sociological Level of Analysis

At the sociological level, the group is the relevant unit of analysis; the individual actor does not play a prominent role at this level of analysis. He is of concern only to the extent to which he is added with others to form a group.

A representation of the sociological level of analysis is provided in the first diagram of Figure 1.1. The large circles portray social groups, while the small circles stand for the people belonging to a given group. Lines indicate the nature of interac-

Wiley & Sons, Inc., 1964); Bernard R. Berelson, Paul F. Lazarsfeld, and William N. McPhee, *Voting* (Chicago: University of Chicago Press, 1954); Angus Campbell, Gerald Gurin, and Warren Miller, *The Voter Decides* (Evanston: Row, Peterson and Co., 1954); William H. Flanigan, *Political Behavior of the American Electorate* (Boston: Allyn and Bacon, Inc., 1968); V. O. Key, Jr., *The Responsible Electorate* (New York: Vintage Books, 1968); Paul Lazarsfeld, Bernard Berelson, and Hazel Gaudet, *The People's Choice* (New York: Duell, Sloan and Pearce, 1944).
[2] See Berelson, *et al.*, *Voting*, Chapter 10.

FIGURE 1.1
THEORETICAL LEVELS OF ANALYSIS

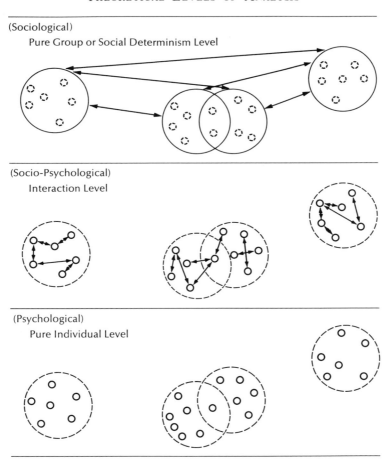

(Sociological)
  Pure Group or Social Determinism Level

(Socio-Psychological)
  Interaction Level

(Psychological)
  Pure Individual Level

tion. Solid lines represent important aspects of the system, and broken lines depict less relevant objects and relationships. It is possible, of course, for a person to belong to more than one group.

The diagram emphasizes two important facts about the group

level of analysis. First, the solid lines used for the groups (large circles) demonstrate the weight attached to the group as an object of concern. Second, the relevant kind of interaction occurs among groups rather than individuals.

This analytical framework is found in much of the group theory literature of political science. Many writers [3] believe that Arthur F. Bentley,[4] whose work concentrates on the interests and demands of groups, is the purest representative of this intellectual heritage.

David Truman, another scholar who has made a significant contribution to group theory in political science,[5] concentrates on explanations of political activity stated in terms of group behavior. A group, in this instance, is a collectivity of individuals with shared interests, which, in turn, provides the basis for acting together.

The sociological level of analysis has also found its way into the voting behavior literature. For example, in Lazarsfeld, *et al., The People's Choice,* considerable effort is expended upon the examination of the relationship between social categorizations and partisan loyalty. This pursuit reflects the sociological or "social determinism" approach to the study of electoral behavior.

Voter decision-making models representing this level of analysis are found in Pool, *et al., Candidates, Issues & Strategies.*[6] The simulations incorporated in this research project will be reviewed in a later chapter.

---

[3] Among others, see R. E. Dowling, "Pressure Group Theory: Its Methodological Range," *American Political Science Review,* Vol. LIV, No. 4 (December 1960), pp. 944–45.

[4] See Arthur F. Bentley, *The Process of Government* (Chicago: University of Chicago Press, 1908). For a review of Bentley and other group theorists, see Chapter 1 of Harmon Zeigler, *Interest Groups in American Society* (Englewood Cliffs, N.J.: Prentice-Hall, 1964).

[5] See David B. Truman, *The Governmental Process* (New York: Alfred A. Knopf, 1951).

[6] Ithiel de Sola Pool, Robert P. Abelson, and Samuel Popkin, *Candidates Issues & Strategies: A Computer Simulation of the 1960 and 1964 Presidential Elections* (Cambridge, Mass.: The M.I.T. Press, 1964).

Socio-Psychological Level of Analysis

As indicated by the second diagram in Figure 1.1, the socio-psychological level of analysis places primary emphasis upon the individual as the relevant analytical unit. To appreciate behavioral dynamics, one must observe individual activity. However, a very important qualification must be added to this definition. The scholar must consider individuals as they *interact* with others. The importance of this interaction is indicated in Figure 1.1 by the solid lines connecting the individuals (small circles). Although the interaction of individuals is the major concern, the group is quite relevant insofar as it provides the social context within which interaction occurs.

A good deal of intellectual background for this approach is found in the literature on primary or small group behavior.[7] Of particular importance is the general conclusion of the literature on political socialization that party identification is learned in the family.[8] One explanation for this phenomenon is that the acquisition of party identification is a function of the personal interaction taking place in the family.

The model that best represents this level of analysis is employed by William N. McPhee and his associates.[9] Their voting

[7] For example, see Sidney Verba, *Small Groups and Political Behavior: A Study of Leadership* (Princeton: Princeton University Press, 1961); and Elihu Katz and Paul F. Lazarsfeld, *Personal Influence* (New York: The Free Press, 1955).

[8] For example, see Herbert Hyman, *Political Socialization* (Glencoe: The Free Press, 1959); Kenneth P. Langton, *Political Socialization* (New York: Oxford University Press, 1969); David Easton and Jack Dennis, *Children in the Political System: Origins of Political Legitimacy* (New York: McGraw-Hill, 1969); Robert D. Hess and Judith V. Torney, *The Development of Political Attitudes in Children* (Chicago: Aldine Publishing Company, 1967).

[9] William N. McPhee and Robert B. Smith, "A Model for Analyzing Voting Systems," in William N. McPhee and William Glaser (eds.), *Public Opinion and Congressional Elections* (New York: The Free Press of Glencoe, 1962), pp. 123–54; William N. McPhee and Jack Ferguson, "Political Immunization," in William N. McPhee and William Glaser (eds.), *Public Opinion and Congressional Elections* (New York: The Free Press of Glencoe, 1962), pp. 155–79; Jack Ferguson and Robert

simulations, which are reported here in several places, rely heavily upon primary group theory, and at the same time deal with the group as the setting for meaningful interaction. This voter decision-making model will also be discussed in a later chapter.

Psychological Level of Analysis

The final level of analysis depicted in Figure 1.1 is the psychological approach. Here, emphasis shifts to the calculations made by individuals without any specific reference to group behavior. The diagram (Fig. 1.1) also indicates that interaction is not a chief consideration at this level of analysis.

One treatment of political behavior which exemplifies the psychological approach is Harold Lasswell's *Psychopathology and Politics*. In this work, Lasswell relates individual psychosexual drives to political action. However, one need not concentrate on emotional or neurotic aspects of political man to deal with the individual or psychological level of analysis. In fact, two distinct models of voter decision-making utilize the individual as the relevant object of concern without making any allusions to the non-rational side of human behavior. One of these theoretical models is Anthony Downs's, *An Economic Theory of Democracy*,[10] while the other is the Survey Research Center's six-component model. Both of these models will be discussed later, and they will also be empirically tested by the technique of computer simulation.

Conclusion

It should be stressed that no theory is a pure representation of a given mode of analysis as defined above. However, the mod-

Smith, "A Theory of Informal Social Influence," in William N. McPhee (ed.), *Formal Theories of Mass Behavior* (New York: The Free Press of Glencoe, 1963), pp. 74–99; and William N. McPhee, "Note on a Campaign Simulator," *Public Opinion Quarterly*, Vol. XXV, No. 2 (1961), pp. 184–93.

[10] Anthony Downs, *An Economic Theory of Democracy* (New York: Harper, 1957).

els of voting behavior subjected to computer simulation can be classified at these theoretical levels on the basis of their major emphasis. The Simulmatics approach, for example, represents the sociological level of analysis, while McPhee's simulations demonstrate socio-psychological or interaction theory. In turn, the Downsian and SRC models can be readily classified at the psychological level of analysis.

Since all of these voter models have been analyzed through the use of computer simulation, it is necessary to provide a general discussion of simulation as a research method before turning to its application to the respective models.

2 Computer simulation as a research technique

In very general terms simulation refers to an attempt to imitate a process which occurs in the empirical world. Successful representation of a process allows the researcher to observe the simulated version of reality and to draw inferences regarding the impact of various parameters on real-world behavior.

The use of simulation need not be confined to any one academic discipline. Even within the social sciences, the simulation strategy has enjoyed a wide and varied usage. The elaborate definition of simulation offered by Richard E. Dawson will generally encompass any social science applications:

> Simulation, as a social science research technique, refers to the construction and manipulation of an *operating* model, that model being a physical or symbolic representation of all or some aspects of a social or psychological process. Simulation, for the social scientist, is the building of an operating model of an individual or group process and experimenting on this replication by manipulating its variables and their interrelationships.[1]

[1] Richard E. Dawson, "Simulation in the Social Sciences," in Harold Guetzkow (ed.), *Simulation in Social Science: Readings* (Englewood Cliffs, N.J.: Prentice-Hall, 1962), p. 3.

Simulation has been employed in many areas of concern to the various disciplines within the social sciences including the economy,[2] artificial intelligence,[3] personality,[4] cognitive processes,[5] international relations,[6] and legislative behavior.[7]

The technique of simulation is attractive in these domains because it provides an opportunity to analyze complex social and psychological processes. Increasing size and complexity of any given process model virtually necessitate the use of simulation as the appropriate research tool. Furthermore, the resulting flexibility enlarges the creative capacity of the scientist in his search for meaningful explanations of the processes of human behavior.

A so-called process model may originate in an existing theory or a systematic combination of aspects of real-world behavior. The resulting model can be represented pictorially. Such a schematic expression of a process model is referred to as a "flow chart." This flow chart or flow diagram summarizes behavior as it is hypothesized to occur over time. Some researchers view flow charts as the basis for an alternative to mathematical models.

A model based on a flow chart may be called an information processing model, to distinguish it from a mathematical model.

[2] See Guy H. Orcutt, "Simulation of Economic Systems," *The American Economic Review,* Vol. I, No. 5 (1960), pp. 893–907.

[3] See Marvin L. Minsky, "Artificial Intelligence," *Scientific American,* Vol. 215 (September 1966), pp. 246–60.

[4] See Silvan S. Tomkins and Samuel Messick, *Computer Simulation of Personality* (New York: John Wiley and Sons, 1963).

[5] For example, see Carl I. Hovland, "Computer Simulation of Thinking," *The American Psychologist,* Vol. 15 (1960), pp. 687–93; Allen Newell, J. C. Shaw, and Herbert Simon, "Elements of a Theory of Human Problem Solving," *Psychological Review,* Vol. 65, No. 3 (1958), pp. 151–66; E. A. Feigenbaum and J. Feldman, *Computers and Thought* (New York: McGraw-Hill, 1963); and Walter R. Reitman, *Cognition and Thought* (New York: John Wiley and Sons, 1966).

[6] See Harold Guetzkow, Chadwick F. Alger, Richard A. Brody, and Richard C. Snyder, *Simulation in International Relations: Developments for Research and Teaching* (Englewood Cliffs, N.J.: Prentice-Hall, 1963).

[7] See Michael J. Shapiro, "The House and the Federal Role: A Computer Simulation of Roll-Call Voting," *The American Political Science Review,* Vol. 26 (1968), pp. 494–517.

Flow charts are much more flexible than mathematical equations and are particularly useful in modeling the so-called "higher" mental processes, such as problem-solving, where a complex kind of feedback arrangement must be pictured.[8]

An example of a model based on a flow chart is presented in Figure 2.1. The model actually is a sub-process of Shapiro's recent roll-call voting simulation. The flow diagram describes the process by which Congressmen arrive at an original predisposition toward a given piece of legislation. During this "predisposition phase," the legislator weighs his attitude toward a bill in accordance with his existing policy orientations, partisan and state loyalties, his own legislative involvement with the bill, and constituency and regional orientations. This summation procedure generates an original predisposition, which becomes the input to other sub-processes of the overall model.

The manner in which elements of a given model are interrelated permits one to ascertain whether the model is primarily *deterministic* or *stochastic*. A deterministic model would state that if event A occurs, then event B will also take place. On the other hand, if a stochastic model is being employed, the relationship is structured quite differently. In this instance, the simulation would state that if event A occurs, the probability is X that event B will also come to pass.

To illustrate this point, one need only turn to the second stage of the Shapiro model (see Fig. 2.2). This sub-process is described as the "predisposition-communication linkage" stage of the model. During this phase, the decision is made as to whether the legislator will enter into "communication" with other political actors.

Figure 2.2 indicates that if a Congressman surpasses a certain level of positive attitudinal intensity he will vote for the bill. Conversely, a similar negative orientation leads directly to a final vote against the bill. If the legislator maintains a moderate initial predisposition, he then enters into communication with other relevant political actors. The simulation of this decision is thus *deterministic* in nature. If the Congressman holds a

---

[8] Bert F. Green, Jr., *Digital Computers in Research* (New York: McGraw-Hill, 1963), p. 196.

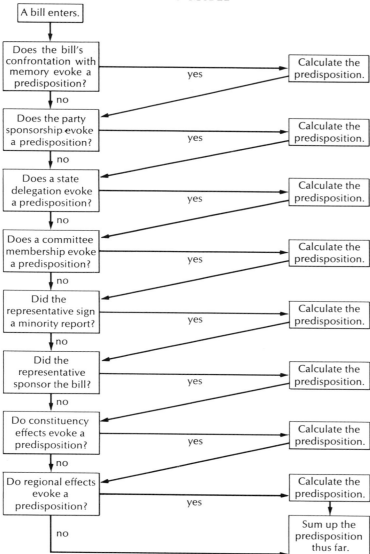

FIGURE 2.1
"PREDISPOSITION PHASE" OF SHAPIRO'S ROLL-CALL VOTING MODEL

A bill enters.

Does the bill's confrontation with memory evoke a predisposition? — yes → Calculate the predisposition.

no

Does the party sponsorship evoke a predisposition? — yes → Calculate the predisposition.

no

Does a state delegation evoke a predisposition? — yes → Calculate the predisposition.

no

Does a committee membership evoke a predisposition? — yes → Calculate the predisposition.

no

Did the representative sign a minority report? — yes → Calculate the predisposition.

no

Did the representative sponsor the bill? — yes → Calculate the predisposition.

no

Do constituency effects evoke a predisposition? — yes → Calculate the predisposition.

no

Do regional effects evoke a predisposition? — yes → Calculate the predisposition.

no

Sum up the predisposition thus far.

Source: Michael J. Shapiro, "The House and the Federal Role: A Computer Simulation of Roll-Call Voting," *The American Political Science Review*, Vol. 621, No. 2 (1968), p. 495.

FIGURE 2.2
"LINKAGE" PHASE OF SHAPIRO'S ROLL-CALL
VOTING MODEL

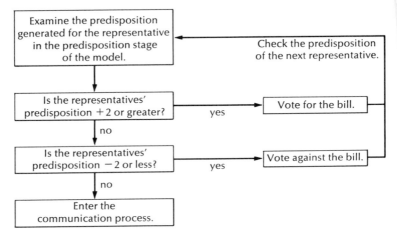

Source: Michael J. Shapiro, "The House and the Federal Role: A Computer Simulation of Roll-Call Voting," *ibid.*, p. 498.

certain level of attitude intensity, then it follows that he will vote for (or against) the bill.

> Only those representatives whose predispositions fall within the range between plus two and minus two enter the communication process to be influenced. The final votes of all others are *determined* in the predisposition phase of the model.[9]

Had this decision been modeled stochastically, the relationship could be stated as follows: if the Congressman holds a certain level of attitude intensity, the probability is X that he will vote for (or against) the bill. If the result of a subsequent probabilistic calculation for a legislator beyond the plus two—minus two range dictates against a decision at the predisposition phase, the legislator will enter communication. In other words,

[9] Michael J. Shapiro, "The House and the Federal Role: A Computer Simulation of Roll-Call Voting," p. 497. My italics.

those who maintain strong positions will have a certain, albeit small, probability of entering into communication.

The appropriateness of either a deterministic or a stochastic approach is a decision which must be made by the researcher. In the example above, does the legislator always have some probability of interacting with his colleagues on a certain bill, or, when his opinions are strong enough, does he cross a threshold which automatically triggers a final decision for or against a bill? If the researcher has a probabilistic explanation of the interaction process, then he will employ a stochastic model. However, if the process has a non-probabilistic interpretation, then a deterministic approach is utilized.

The preceding discussion indicated that a stochastic procedure is reflected in the statement, if A occurs, then the probability is X that event B will also occur. This may very well be a meaningful way of stating sequential events. However, in any given simulation, how does the researcher know when B will actually take place? If X is the probability that a legislator will communicate with his colleagues, then on any given test of the model, how does one decide whether or not the legislator actually does interact with those around him? One useful answer to this question is to be found in the Monte Carlo method which employs probability and random number generation to determine whether or not an event will occur.

> In effect we have turned probability theory onto itself. One of the goals of probability theory is to describe the distribution of probability numbers over events. Our goal to create events by generating probability numbers is just the reverse. While probability theory proceeds from events to probabilities, Monte Carlo simulation proceeds from probabilities to events. One purpose is the inverse of the other.[10]

Consequently, the Monte Carlo method offers a solution based upon a utilization of random numbers. If the researcher can generate random numbers between 0.0 and 1.0, then he can

---

[10] Richard F. Barton, *A Primer on Simulation and Gaining* (Englewood Cliffs, N.J.: Prentice-Hall, 1970), p. 152.

decide whether or not a sequence *actually* transpires in the model. For the above hypothetical legislative situation, the probability that the Congressman will communicate with others may be .7. In other words, 70 per cent of the range of random numbers will lead to discussion, while the remaining 30 per cent of all random numbers will not produce discussion. Thus, if one randomly generates a number of .4, discussion will ensue. On the other hand, if .93 is randomly produced, interaction will not occur for that legislator. It is self-evident that the Monte Carlo method is a key means of using stochastic processes.

Another technique employed in simulation involves the use of heuristics. Unlike algorithms, which give solutions to problems by making calculations of every possible contingency, heuristic devices act as "rules of thumb." Heuristics have been particularly helpful in simulating cognitive processes. For example, consider the

> . . . logic-theory machine of Newell, Shaw, and Simon, which produced proofs of theorems in logical calculus. Rather than using an all-inclusive algorithm for proving logic theorems, their program used a set of *heuristics:* rules of thumb which usually work in producing proofs but which have no guarantee of success. The heuristics were represented in the program by a list of possibilities: heuristics that worked were moved up on the list, while unsuccessful heuristics were demoted.[11]

Another example involves the Downsian rational actor. Rather than explore every possible effect a given party might have on utility flows, the voter in the Downsian model may use a heuristic device, such as party identification, to simplify the task of judging the merits of the party under consideration. He may find that such rules of thumb work quite well. Success then ensures that he will be conditioned to use this heuristic device on other occasions.

In real-world situations, of course, human beings use mental rules of thumb to solve problems rather than consider every

---

[11] Bert F. Green, Jr., *Digital Computers in Research,* p. 97.

conceivable possibility. In fact, algorithmic solutions may be impossible to achieve in most human problem-solving ventures. Therefore, heuristic procedures are useful shortcuts in decision-making. Nevertheless, heuristics are not necessarily infallible, even if they seem to work fairly well.

One of the most creative aspects of the simulation technique is "sensitivity testing."

> The exploration of the relative importance of different parts of the model is technically called "sensitivity testing." Sensitivity testing is one of the more important uses of computer simulation. One often designs a computer model not for the purpose of predicting but for the purpose of gaining an understanding of the process represented. By varying each of the parameters of the model one can see which ones make a difference and which ones do not. Some few variables may account for little. To explore the sensitivity of the prediction to the value of each parameter is one way of gaining a deeper understanding of what is taking place.[12]

Sensitivity testing, therefore, facilitates "experiments" on real-life situations. By systematically altering the relative importance of the various parameters in a model, the researcher may be able to gain significant insights into the overall process being studied.

Finally, one should note that the present study addresses itself to *computer* simulations of voting behavior. With increasing size and complexity of a theoretical model, combined with large numbers of voters, it becomes infeasible to simulate voter decision-making processes without the assistance of a computer.

In order to take full advantage of the computer's capabilities, the theoretical model expressed in a flow chart must be translated into a computer program.

> For a flow chart to achieve precision, it must become the basis of a working computer program. Without a program, there is no way to tell whether or not the chart specifies the process ex-

---

[12] Pool, Abelson, and Popkin, *Candidates, Issues & Strategies,* pp. 64–65.

actly, for all possible contingencies. *The program, rather than the flow chart, is the model.*[13]

The computer, then, makes it possible to examine large, complex models with relative ease. Furthermore, Monte Carlo methods and sensitivity testing provide realistic solutions when the researcher can exploit the speed and precision of the computer.

In assessing how well a given simulation model approximates the actual process, one most often *evaluates the simulation in light of the accuracy with which the model predicts actual behavior.* This will be the principal criterion adopted in this study.

[13] Bert F. Green, Jr., *Digital Computers in Research,* p. 197. My italics.

3 Models of voter decision-making

Voter Simulation at the Sociological Level of Analysis

Computer simulation of voting behavior using the "sociological" level of analysis was usefully employed by Pool, Abelson, and Popkin, who first applied their technique of simulation to the 1960 presidential election.[1] Prior to the campaign, Edward Greenfield, an active New York Democrat, raised a substantial amount of interest in the project within the Democratic Party, later translated into financial support from the Democratic Advisory Council, which had an abiding concern in securing information having direct application to the problems encountered during the campaign. In order to provide an organizational framework for the execution of their research, the analysts, who were associated with the Massachusetts Institute of Technology, established the Simulmatics Corporation.

The Simulmatics Project's basic theoretical framework relies heavily upon an assumption of social determinism. Empirical evidence can be gathered to demonstrate that certain socioeconomic groups have a tendency to favor one political party over another. Therefore, it is assumed that certain kinds of political behavior, in this case voting, are a function of membership in

[1] For the simulations of the 1960 and 1964 elections, see Pool, Abelson, and Popkin, *Candidates, Issues & Strategies*.

one or more identifiable social or economic categories.[2] The following statements reflect social determinism: Catholics have a tendency to vote Democratic; Protestants tend to vote Republican; labor union members tend to vote Democratic; urban dwellers tend to vote Democratic; and college educated individuals tend to vote Republican.

Several factors may account for this empirical phenomenon. Historical antecedents are often the cause of consistency. The Republican Party, as the party of Lincoln, attracted large numbers of black voters. In the era of the New Deal and Franklin D. Roosevelt, the historical pattern was redefined in such a way that the Democrats now clearly have the electoral support of black Americans.

If historical patterns and self-interest are not sufficient reasons for the maintenance of voting consistency by social groups, we may assume that certain processes take place which may generate a greater degree of conformity in the individual to the social group. Pool, Abelson, and Popkin make this point by stating that

> . . . when social milieu and political views are out of balance, then further adjustment processes may be set in motion. The voter may compromise his views toward those of his friends, or attempt to convince his friends of the merit of his own views. Failing this, he may manage to misperceive his friends' views to produce the illusion of consensus. . . . Lastly, if a person finds that his friends' political (and other) views are uncongenial, he may try to find new friends whose views are more congenial.[3]

Of course, the reader is well aware that socio-economic groups generally do not demonstrate complete consistency in

[2] Such empirical evidence has been a part of many important voting studies. The relationship of political party to socio-economic class is given considerable attention in Lazarsfeld, Berelson, and Gaudet. *The People's Choices.* Furthermore, this relationship has been a part of most major voting studies. For example, see Berlson, Lazarsfeld, and McPhee, *Voting;* Campbell, Gurin, and Miller, *The Voter Decides;* Campbell, Converse, Miller, and Stokes, *The American Voter.*

[3] Pool, Abelson, and Popkin, *Candidates, Issues & Strategies,* p. 11.

their voting patterns. Any given group may display a tendency toward supporting a political party, but a substantial minority of that group may deviate from the general pattern. For example, it may very well be true that Protestants tend to vote Republican. Nevertheless, it would not be difficult to marshal a sufficient amount of statistical evidence to indicate that a sizable proportion of Protestants also vote Democratic. The same can be said of other social groups. Many blue-collar workers vote Republican. Large numbers of college graduates vote Democratic, etc.

The empirical observation that there are exceptions to a general tendency within a socio-economic group to vote for the same party, provides the basic element of "cross-pressure" theory. "Cross pressures" refer to

> . . . combinations of characteristics which in a given context, would tend to lead the individual to vote on both sides of a contest. A variety of cross pressures can be distinguished. The probability of a person's vote . . . is affected, as we have seen, by his position in the social structure, by his former party allegiance, and by the specific appeals of the campaign. Any two of these factors predisposing him in different directions can lead to cross pressures. In addition, his social position alone can create cross pressure (e.g., in recent elections, a rich Catholic); and so can his stand on various issues (e.g., an isolationist New Dealer).[4]

According to "cross-pressure" theory, when an individual is predisposed to vote for the preference of his socio-economic group, he will be able to make a decision more easily. Associating with people demographically like himself, the voter derives support from his immediate social environment. This supportive social milieu reinforces a decision that may have been the individual's original choice. There is no particular reason to believe that the voter necessarily arrived at a position only later to seek support of those around him. On the contrary, he may very well have received important cues from individuals in similar circumstances before his decision was made. Regardless of

[4] Berelson, *et al., Voting,* pp. 283–84.

the origin of a decision, consistency within an individual's constellation of socio-economic attachments tends to simplify the process considerably.

Without in-group cohesiveness, many individual members of the group would experience "cross pressures." These "cross pressures" would be seen to have various effects upon voting behavior. Generally speaking,

> An individual who is characterized by any type of cross pressure is likely to change his mind in the course of the campaign, to make up his mind late, and, occasionally, to leave the field and not to vote at all.[5]

Nevertheless, even people under cross pressures demonstrate a "tendency toward consistency." In other words, people who are "inconsistent," usually support their party despite some deviant positions. This "tendency toward consistency" is thought to be generated by increased campaign activity and greater personal attention to politically relevant material.

Applying cross-pressure theory to the 1960 presidential election contest between John F. Kennedy and Richard M. Nixon, Pool, Abelson, and Popkin hypothesized that past voting behavior and attitudes toward a Catholic President were the salient factors affecting the decisions of those in the three religious groups and the three party-identification classifications. If one cross-classifies the socio-economic categories of religion and party, several combinations could be created.

As indicated by the X's in Figure 3.1, the two primary instances of cross pressure were Catholic Republicans and Protestant Democrats. With the candidacy of John F. Kennedy, the question of electing a Catholic President became relevant for many people. Large numbers of Catholic Republicans shifted to support a Catholic, while many Protestant Democrats abandoned the Democratic Party and its Roman Catholic nominee. Consequently, the nine combinations represented in Figure 3.1 became the basis for the 1960 Simulmatics model. Voting patterns were assumed to be a result of group consistencies and

[5] *Ibid.*, p. 284.

FIGURE 3.1
CROSS-PRESSURE PATTERN

	Republicans	Democrats	Independents
Protestants		X	
Catholics	X		
Others*			

* Jews and blacks of all religions. The Protestants and Catholic groups consist of whites only. Reprinted from page 46 of *Candidates, Issues & Strategies,* by Ithiel de Sola Pool, Robert B. Abelson, and Samuel Popkin by permission of the M.I.T. Press, Cambridge, Mass. Copyright 1964 and 1965 by the Massachusetts Institute of Technology.

cross pressures. We shall return to this theoretical model after briefly considering the data processing aspects of the project.

The data used for the computer simulations were responses to sixty-five national surveys, administered in the pre-election periods of 1952, 1954, 1956, 1958, and 1960. Initially, fifty surveys, incorporating information from 100,000 respondents for the 1952–58 period, represented the basic data. Pre-1960 surveys were added to the data bank as they became available. When completed, the data bank included 130,000 respondents. The Roper Public Opinion Research Center released these surveys to the project with the proviso that the data be made available to the Republican Party upon request, and that all results of scientific import could be published after the campaign.

These survey data were organized into a 480 x 52 matrix. The 480 axis represented the number of voter-types, as defined by region of the country, socio-economic status, city size, sex, religious affiliation, and ethnicity.[6] Therefore, one of the 480 voter-types could be Eastern, Democratic, Catholic, white, male, urban, blue-collar worker. Another classification would be Southern, Democratic, Protestant, Negro, male, rural, blue-collar worker.

For each voter-type, the attitudinal distributions on each of

[6] Regional categories were East, South, Midwest, and Border. For states included for each division, see Pool, Abelson, and Popkin, *Candidates, Issues & Strategies,* p. 27. For specifics on other characteristics, see Table 1.1 in Pool, Abelson, and Popkin, pp. 28–29.

52 "issue-clusters" (attitudes on policy questions and political characteristics) were computed.[7] For every voter-type, therefore, the researchers calculated the number of people questioned about each "issue" as well as the number of pro, con, and undecided responses recorded on that "issue."

The election predictions made by the Simulmatics Corporation were on a state-by-state basis. This was done primarily because the electoral college uses the state as the relevant unit of concern; no matter how small a statewide plurality, the winner receives all of the state's electoral votes. Since states have different numbers of electoral votes, more meaningful and practical predictions are facilitated by state-by-state simulations. In order to accomplish this task, they had to create "synthetic states."

> By an elaborate analysis of census, poll, and voting data . . .
> we developed a set of estimates on the number of persons of
> each voter-type in each state. It was assumed that a voter of a
> given voter-type would be identical regardless of the state from
> which he came. A synthetic state therefore consisted of a
> weighted average of the voter-types in that state, the weighting
> being proportional to the numbers of such persons in that
> state. For example, we assumed that the difference between
> Maine and New York is not truly a difference between New
> Yorkers and inhabitants of Maine as such, *but a difference in
> the proportions of voter-types which make up each state.*[8]

With the completion of the data organization, the researchers were ready to begin simulating the 1960 election. As alluded to above, the 480 voter-types were classified according to past voting behavior and religion. The two cross-pressured groups were Catholic Republicans and Protestant Democrats.

For each group represented by the nine cells of the above-cited "cross-pressure pattern" table, a prediction was made of the percentages of voters with preferences for Kennedy and Nixon. The criteria for these voting estimates were as follows:

---

[7] For a list of the 52 "issues," see Table 1.2 in Pool, Abelson, and Popkin, pp. 32–33.

[8] *Ibid.,* pp. 40–41. My italics.

1. Protestant Republicans were expected to repeat the partisan voting pattern they displayed in the 1956 presidential election.

2. Protestant Democrats were predicted to extend their normal proportion of votes to the Democratic Party minus that percentage having reservations about a Catholic President. Such a negative attitude toward having a Catholic in the White House was labelled "anti-Catholicism."

3. Protestant Independents were treated in the same manner as Protestant Democrats.

4. Catholic Republicans would have a tendency to abandon their usual voting habits because a Catholic was running on the Democratic ticket. One-third of this group was expected to abandon the Republican Party. This type of vote-switching was referred to as the "Catholic shift."

5. Catholic Democrats were expected to increase their normal support of the Democratic Party by one-third, since their religion and party loyalty were mutually reinforcing.

6. Catholic Independents were predicted to modify their typical voting pattern in the same manner as Catholic Democrats.

7. Other Republicans would act the same as Catholic Republicans because Jewish and black voters would consider an attack on Kennedy's religion to be somewhat distasteful.

8. Other Democrats would decrease their usual support for the Democratic Party by that percentage who maintained "anti-Catholic" sentiments.

9. Other Independents were treated in essentially the same way as Other Democrats.

These criteria were expressed in mathematical equations which were utilized to estimate the percentage of Democratic and Republican support by each voter-type. These prognostications were weighted by the percentage of past non-voting of the specific voter-type being considered. Of course, voters who were cross-pressured were assigned lower turnout rates than might normally be expected.

Within any given "synthetic state," the percentage of Kennedy voters of a given voter-type was applied to the number of that voter-type in order to determine the number of Kennedy voters. The same procedure was employed for Nixon voters. After applying this technique to each voter-type, Kennedy and Nixon votes could be tallied, thereby yielding the statewide predictions. The supposed "winner" would then be assigned the electoral votes of that state. The "synthetic state" results were then totaled to yield the simulated electoral vote division.

Pool, Abelson, and Popkin initially applied their simulation model to thirty-two non-Southern states. The correlation between actual state results and the predicted outcomes of the computer simulation (product moment correlation) was .82, which means that the simulation predictions account for 67.24 per cent of the variance of the actual electoral results, leaving one-third of the variance unexplained. For this particular test of the model, all survey data through 1958 were utilized.

The next theoretical concern was to explore the impact of various parameters of the model. This was accomplished by a process previously defined as "sensitivity testing." The first parameter subjected to sensitivity testing was religion. Removing the "anti-Catholicism" cluster had the effect of lowering the correlation of the original model from .82 to .62. In other words, without the anti-Catholicism factor, the simulated results explained 38.44 per cent of the variance in actual statewide election returns.

It must be recalled that an assumption was made that Catholics would shift from the Republican Party to the Democratic Party. This Catholic voting shift was to include one-third of all Catholic Republicans. By varying the weight of the Catholic-shift parameter between 0.1 and 1.0, it was found that the correlation between simulated and actual results remained fairly constant. However, the dispersion (the square root of the mean-square error) was definitely lowest when the Catholic shift was set at .7.

Simultaneous variation of both the "anti-Catholicism" and "Catholic-shift" parameters produced interesting results. Dropping both components from the model gave predictions having only a .50 correlation with actual outcomes. Therefore, simulated results explained 25 per cent of the variance in actual statewide patterns. Eliminating the "anti-Catholicism" dimension from the model, while retaining the "Catholic-shift" factor, resulted in a good correlation, if the "Catholic shift" was between 80 and 100 per cent. *The ultimate conclusion revealed by testing this parameter was that the simulation was highly sensitive to the religious factor.*

Sensitivity testing was then applied to the participation parameter. The results of using various methods of estimating voter turnout showed

> . . . that the best alternative was to use no turnout information at all. Although the correlation coefficients are the same in all cases, any use of turnout information increased the average error substantially by lowering the Democratic vote.[9]

This finding led to what is perhaps the most important substantive theoretical conclusion coming out of the Simulmatics research project.

> The failure of a turnout correction to improve the results is not a trivial finding. It is a finding in direct contradiction to a major social science theory that we and others have used and accepted for a good many years. It contradicts the proposition that persons under cross pressure vote less than others.[10]

Actually, this observation is not intended to be a rejection of "cross-pressure" theory. Instead, it implies modification of the theory. The hypothesis of increased non-voting for cross-pressured groups was first stated in *Voting*. However, cross pressure in the 1948 election resulted from *negative* feelings toward both candidates. In terms of conflict theory jargon, this means that an "avoidance-avoidance" conflict, which normally leads to non-voting, was established. On the other hand, in 1960 Republican Catholics were *attracted* by Kennedy, while many Protestants were *attracted* to Nixon in order to satisfy their "anti-Catholic" attitudes. The 1960 election, therefore, created an "approach-approach" conflict for millions of voters. With positive attractions to both candidates, those cross pressured

---

[9] *Ibid.*, p. 73.
[10] *Ibid.*, pp. 74–75.

would remain in the "field" and reduce the "conflict" by choosing between Kennedy and Nixon rather than resolve the "conflict" through non-voting as was the case in 1948. "At any rate, we can say with confidence that the simple theory that postulates non-voting as the outcome of cross pressure can no longer be maintained." [11]

The authors also attempted simulations based upon two areas of concern—foreign policy and civil rights. Employing a model using attitudes on foreign policy as the determining factor provided results which correlated with actual election returns at .43. The authors concluded that foreign policy attitudes were not decisive in generating voting preferences. Essentially the same conclusion is reached for the civil rights simulation. Focusing upon Northern states, a civil rights model yielded predictions that correlated with actual returns at .41. The product moment correlation for all forty-eight states was .47 (Alaska and Hawaii were not included in the analysis). In general, *foreign policy and civil rights attitudes were not key factors in the 1960 presidential election.*

The final simulation of the 1960 election is an attempt to set the parameter values so as to give the best results. By choosing parameters to best fit the actual outcomes, one may produce simulations which help provide an explanation of what happened in the real world.

To achieve the "best fit" of the simulation to the election returns, Pool, Abelson, and Popkin made the following changes in their 1960 model:

1. We dropped the turnout correction factor that had added nothing to the accuracy of our prediction.

2. We used the 5-period instead of the 4-period master deck of data.

3. We assumed a shift to Kennedy of .4 of Catholics who otherwise would have voted Republican. A .3 shift is indeed almost as good and better by some criteria, so this slight departure from the .33 used in 1960 is not really significant.

4. We introduced a new shift in the Southern states only, namely a postulate that 10 percent of Negroes who would oth-

[11] *Ibid.,* p. 78.

erwise have voted for Nixon voted for Kennedy, and 10 percent of whites who would otherwise have voted for Kennedy voted for Nixon.[12]

The product moment correlation between these simulation predictions and state-by-state returns is .81 for thirty-two Northern states. This represents no real change from the product moment correlation of the first model which was .82. The authors claim, however, that the South's simulated voting patterns become more consistent with electoral reality. For all forty-eight states, the product moment correlation is .70. The "best-fit" simulation also yields predictions characterized by a very small absolute departure [13] from actual election results.

From the Simulmatics Corporation's perspective, the 1960 election outcome depended upon two principal factors: *party* and *religion*. Party identification, which is most efficacious in determining voting in Congressional elections, is also crucial to voting behavior in presidential contests, in spite of the fact that the candidates' personalities do generate sizable shifts in party voting.

The religious issue in 1960 caused significant shifts of Protestant Democrats to the Republican Party and Republican Catholics to the Democratic Party. The Simulmatics model offers a most insightful analysis of the religious dimension:

The shift of one in ten American voters on religious grounds cost Kennedy one and a half million votes, or 2.3 percent of the total vote. But while Kennedy lost in popular vote he gained in electoral votes on the religious issue. The best-fit simulation indicates that Kennedy netted 22 electoral votes because of the religious issue! Table 3.4 reveals that bunching of the Catholic shift in large, closely fought, industrial states, and the location of much of the Protestant shift in "safe" Southern states gave Kennedy this net advantage despite a popular vote disadvantage.[14]

[12] *Ibid.*, pp. 106–7.
[13] As measured by the median absolute deviation.
[14] *Ibid.*, p. 117.

In conclusion, using a social determinism and cross-pressure theory model, Pool, Abelson, and Popkin revealed that *party and religion were the primary determinants of the voting results in the 1960 election, with religion costing Kennedy popular votes, but netting him electoral votes. Foreign policy and civil rights attitudes were generally unimportant.*

In 1964, Pool, Abelson, and Popkin utilized a model drastically different from that employed in 1960. Whereas the 1960 model emphasized party and religion, the 1964 simulation relied upon party and attitudes toward civil rights, nuclear responsibility, and social welfare legislation. These elements were combined in three different models, the first of which is called the five-factor model. In addition to civil rights, nuclear responsibility, and social welfare legislation, party identification and turnout rates were built into the model. The logic of the 1964 presidential election simulation is as follows:

> All Democrats except those who were strongly opposed to civil rights would vote for Johnson.
>
> All Republicans would vote for Goldwater except those who supported the Democratic side on at least two out of three issue-clusters, namely civil rights, nuclear responsibility, and social welfare legislation.
>
> All Independents who expressed a clear view on civil rights would vote accordingly; those without a clear view on civil rights would vote in accordance with their views on the other two clusters. In estimating how Independents might divide we would disregard those Independents who expressed no views or whose views were evenly balanced.[15]

This simulation predicted that Lyndon B. Johnson would garner 62 per cent of the vote, a figure which was very close to the 61.4 per cent Johnson finally received. However, the product moment correlation between state-by-state predicted and actual vote results was only .52. In other words, simulated outcomes explained only 27.04 per cent of the variance in the real electoral consequences.

[15] *Ibid.*, p. 167.

To improve the predictability of the original model, the authors added a sixth factor, thereby forming a second model. They found that the western plains states were more Democratic than actual voting patterns could justify. (This seems to result from combining these states with Pacific Coast states in one region.) Therefore, the Democratic vote percentage was decreased by 5 per cent in each of these states. This correction increases the correlation between predicted and actual results from .52 to .63.

The third model of the 1964 election is formed by adding a seventh factor. In two southern states, Alabama and Mississippi, Johnson received no votes. In Alabama, Johnson's name did not appear on the ballot, leaving an open field for Barry Goldwater. Mississippi's response to the Democratic nominee was somewhat different. Even though Lyndon Johnson's name appeared on the ballot, the old-line Democratic Party leadership in Mississippi bolted the national party. The result was not surprising—Johnson received but 13 per cent of Mississippi's vote. This seven-factor model provided a .90 correlation between simulated and actual results. Eighty-one per cent of the variance in state voting patterns was explained. With this final model, the simulation of the 1964 presidential election is quite satisfactory.

Nevertheless, several large deviations appeared. In the first place, Arizona went more heavily for Goldwater and Texas provided a much greater plurality for Johnson than the simulation indicated. This phenomenon may be accounted for by a "native son" mentality in each of the respective states.

Secondly, California deviated markedly from the predicted outcome. Goldwater, although soundly defeated by Johnson in California, may have received substantial "white backlash" strength. Witness the victory of George Murphy over Pierre Salinger, who staunchly opposed Proposition 14 (an anti-open-housing proposition). If racial prejudice had not become salient, Johnson, in all likelihood, would have carried California by an even greater margin.

The only other deviant case worth noting is New England, which gave Johnson a much more convincing victory than the simulation predicted. The authors offer no explanation for this occurrence.

Finally, the simulation estimated that Republican defections to the Johnson bandwagon amounted to one-third of all Republicans. This massive shift combined with the observation that a great variety of people (i.e. Negroes, Jews, white-collar workers, blue-collar workers, etc.) gave vote pluralities to Lyndon Johnson, led the researchers to make the following observation: "Indeed the most dramatic aspect of the 1964 election was the extent to which it was genuinely dominated by issues rather than by social stratification." [16]

In conclusion, it can be fairly stated that the Simulmatics project represents one of the most creative research applications of public opinion data. The simulation models, which were formulated at the "sociological" level of analysis, provide many interesting interpretations. Of particular interest is the impact of religion upon the division of popular and electoral votes in the 1960 presidential election. Furthermore, since other meaningful findings, such as the modification of cross-pressure theory, were forthcoming, this writer believes that there is considerable theoretical justification for utilizing the Simulmatics approach in more and different types of elections.

Voter Simulation at the Socio-Psychological Level of Analysis

In questioning the utility of social determinism, V. O. Key, Jr. and Frank Munger state that such a theoretical orientation can lead the researcher to "equate the people's choice with individual choice." [17] Although voting behavior correlates with group membership, the analyst may overlook significant aspects of individual decision-making by concentrating exclusively upon socio-economic classifications.

---

[16] *Ibid.,* p. 177.

[17] V. O. Key, Jr. and Frank Munger, "Social Determinism and Electoral Decision: The Case of Indiana," in Eugene Burdick and Arthur J. Brodbeck (eds.), *American Voting Behavior* (Glencoe, Ill.: The Free Press, 1959), p. 281.

It should be eminently clear that, for the most part, the "people's choice" was equated with the "individual's choice" in the Simulmatics models. Calculating estimates for demographic categories assumes that the individual and the group decision-making processes are virtually identical. If this assessment is too harsh, then it must certainly be conceded that there exists a fortuitous linkage between the preference of the individual and his socio-economic category. Although the Simulmatics predictions were often quite impressive, the focus on the social group did not fully explicate the factors which bear upon and link individual decisions to overall group behavior.

Recognizing the theoretical difficulties of social determinism, William N. McPhee and his associates have attempted to concentrate upon individual behavior as it occurs within the social milieu. They have constructed a socio-psychological model of voting behavior.[18] Without ignoring the impact of group membership, the authors have constructed an individual decision-making model, which

> . . . lends itself to rapid logical manipulation of sizeable numbers of units ("voters") arranged in complicated structures ("communities") through long sequences of processes ("eras" or "generations").[19]

The overall decision-making process consists of three subprocesses, as indicated in Figure 3.2. In the first place, there is a stimulation process, in which the primary factors are external campaign stimuli (e.g. electioneering propaganda) and partisanship or degree of party identification. This process has the attending consequence of generating an initial preference for a given party and its candidate.

At this point, the individual enters into the second process

---

[18] McPhee and Smith, "A Model for Analyzing Voting Systems," pp. 123–54; McPhee and Ferguson, "Political Immunization," pp. 155–79; Ferguson and Smith, "A Theory of Informal Social Influence," pp. 74–79; and McPhee, *Public Opinion Quarterly,* Vol. XXV, No. 2 (Summer 1961), pp. 184–93.

[19] McPhee and Smith, "A Model for Analyzing Voting Systems," p. 125.

—discussion, mainly with primary groups (e.g. the family). If the individual discovers that his partner disagrees with his initial preference, then he seeks additional stimuli to determine whether or not he or his friend is in error. In the McPhee model agreement between a pair is sufficient for "final" decision.

FIGURE 3.2

FLOW DIAGRAM OF
MCPHEE'S SOCIO-PSYCHOLOGICAL MODEL

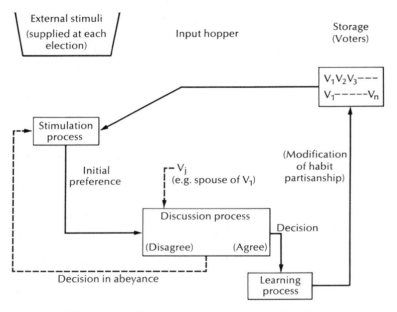

Source: William N. McPhee and Robert B. Smith, "A Model for Analyzing Voting Systems," p. 146.

This ultimate decision is then "learned." It is during this process that the recent partisan choice modifies predispositions which were in existence prior to the election. The new partisanship value is used as the party identification factor for the next election. The reader by this time is well aware that, although the model in Figure 3.2 appears to be quite reasonable, considerable explanation of its operation is required.

Prior to the stimulation process, the voter maintains a certain degree of party identification. The extent of partisanship is merely a probabilistic expression of attachment to the various parties in a given political system. If, for example, one is examining a two-party system, an individual's partisanship ("P") value for one party may be .6, while his "P" value for the other party might be .2. The sum of an individual's partisanship scores must be .9 or less. The range of the "P" values must always be between 0.1 and 0.9 (not 0.0 and 1.0) because there is always the possibility of non-voting.

The calculation of the partisanship index is a simple matter of finding the relative frequency of voting for a given party. The "P" value is therefore nothing more than the percentage of times an individual votes for a party. After the election, the partisanship value is modified during the learning process.

Questions arise as to the status of the individual who has not yet voted. He has no past experience from which to estimate the level of partisanship for the various parties. Therefore, since the model is dependent upon this index, how can a "P" value be calculated for a first voter? In their general description of the model, the authors provide no intuitively satisfying basis for deriving partisanship scores. Instead, for those persons who have not previously voted in an election, the "P" value is arbitrarily set at some number, which is usually low, since the inexperienced participant has not had the opportunity to reinforce a partisan attachment. The arbitrary nature of the initial assignment of "P" values can be circumvented in several ways. Solutions are implied by the general thrust of much of the political socialization literature,[20] which suggests that a majority of children develop a party identification long before they are eligible to vote. Presumably, the intensity of this attitudinal po-

[20] For instance, see Herbert Hyman, *Political Socialization;* Fred I. Greenstein, *Children and Politics* (New Haven: Yale University Press, 1965); Richard Dawson and Kenneth Prewitt, *Political Socialization* (Boston: Little, Brown and Co., 1969); Kenneth P. Langton, *Political Socialization* (New York: Oxford University Press, 1969).

sition could provide the basis for a "P" value.[21] Alternatively, even though pre-voting age citizens are not filing into polling booths, they nevertheless may be engaged in "choosing" their candidate. Such preferences could act as surrogates for actual voting. In any event, empirically valid methods exist for the assignment of "P" values to first voters.

Turning to the question of external stimuli, the type of partisan appeals to the individual is largely a function of his membership in socio-economic groups. For example, college-educated suburbanites probably would be exposed to more Republican stimuli than would urban blue-collar workers. Although the use of socio-economic categories to determine the types of stimuli that an individual is subjected to definitely implies social determinism, in this instance the researchers were not merely observing group tendencies based upon the simple aggregation of individuals. Instead, their use of socio-economic groupings was justified by the fact that *political parties make appeals to groups which are presumed to have importance for individuals.* Consequently, each voter is assigned to some "G" category (or grouping), which is the basis for his receiving partisan stimuli. As the authors state:

> . . . the significant point is that the G categorization of blocs of voters determines which distribution of stimuli these voters will be exposed to from each party during the course of the problem if G is constant, or for successive periods when G is variable (as in problems involving mobility between social categories).[22]

The argument might then be made that since parties direct their propaganda efforts toward certain identifiable groups, surely analysis of voting at the group level should be more than sufficient for an adequate understanding of voting behavior. The answer, of course, is that one still does not have a satisfac-

---

[21] This approach was employed in the application of the model to the 1960 Wisconsin presidential primary. See McPhee, *Public Opinion Quarterly*, Vol. XXV, No. 2 (Summer 1961), pp. 184–93.

[22] McPhee and Smith, "A Model for Analyzing Voting Systems," p. 132.

tory comprehension of the dynamics of *individual* behavior, even if observation at both the group and individual levels yields the same simulation results.

Furthermore, the socio-psychological approach does not ignore the relevance of social groups in order to proceed with analysis of individual behavior. Instead, *interest focuses upon individual behavior as it occurs within the context of social groups.* One is theoretically concerned with the impact of the group upon the individual. McPhee and his associates, therefore, hypothesize that one effect of socio-economic categories is to determine the nature of partisan appeals aimed at the individual voter.

Each "G" categorization has an associated distribution of stimuli for each party, which summarizes the probabilities of receiving all levels of stimulation, ranging from the weakest (1) to the strongest (10).[23]

An example of such a stimulus distribution is presented in Figure 3.3. Such a stimulus intensity table, which may be unique to one group for one party, is actually stored in the computer. To select the strength of the stimulus, a random number generator produces a value ranging from 0.0 to 1.0. This probability is then found in the stimulus intensity table (second column), and the associated symbol of stimulus strength (third column) is used for the amount of stimulation the individual experiences. For example, suppose that the hypothetical table is the Democratic party stimulus distribution for blue-collar workers (the "G" categorization). If the random number which is generated is .17, then the individual receives a stimulus strength of 2. This process would be repeated for other blue-collar workers. Other "G" categorizations, such as white-collar workers, would have different stimulus intensity tables for the Democratic Party.

In addition, the stimulus intensity table represented in Figure

[23] The stimulus strength of each issue of the 1960 Wisconsin presidential primary was inferred by having respondents from each of twenty homogeneous social groups rate every item in terms of its "strength" or "weakness" of appeal. Each social group had a set of distinct stimulus symbols for each issue.

FIGURE 3.3

STIMULUS INTENSITY TABLE
STORED IN COMPUTER

Probability (of each occurring)	Interval (Cumulative Probability)	Symbol (Stimulus Strength) *
.10	.00	1 (weakest)
	.09	
.10	.10	2
	.19	
.10	.20	3
	.29	
.	.	.
.	.	.
.	.	.
.	.	.
.10	.90	10 (strongest)
	.99	

* For "Choice" and "Interest" Computations the symbols are made to vary from 0.1 to 1.0.

Source: William N. McPhee and Robert B. Smith, "A Model for Analyzing Voting Systems," p. 134.

3.3 contains *equal probabilities for all levels of stimuli*. However, in reality, many groups will have *unequal* intervals of stimulus probability. For example, the first interval may comprise the first three levels of cumulative probabilities in the hypothetical table. If this were the Republican Party stimulus distribution for blue-collar workers, then there would be a .3 probability that a blue-collar worker would receive the weakest Republican stimulus (1). As before, the probability is randomly generated by the computer. Likewise, certain "G" categorizations may be high stimulus groups. Consequently, blue-collar workers may have a .4 probability of receiving the strongest Democratic Party stimulus (10). For any given research problem these probabilities could be derived empirically. However, the analyst may want to assign the probabilities arbitrarily for "experimenting" with the model.

At any rate, the stimulus intensity distributions consist of the probabilities of occurrence associated with each level of stimulus strength. A separate table would exist for each political party for each group.

The factors of *partisanship* and *external stimuli* are the basic elements which come into play during the stimulation process. Together, they provide a mechanism for determining individual choice and the level of interest in the campaign. The degree of partisanship has a critical relationship to the strength of external stimuli. The stimulation process of the overall model relies heavily upon the assumption that

> . . . the stronger the person's internal predisposition . . . toward some class of objects (for example, candidates of a party), the weaker the external stimulation required from any such object to elicit a "yes" choice of it by this person. Conversely, the weaker the internal disposition, the stronger must be the external appeal (here strength of stimulus) in order to elicit the "yes" choice.[24]

Therefore, a "strong Democrat" needs very little Democratic Party stimulation to vote for his party. He may even vote for an unpopular Democrat. On the other hand, a "weak Democrat" needs strong stimulation to choose the Democratic candidate. Consequently, there is a greater likelihood that the less loyal Democrat would desert what would ordinarily be the party of his choice.

This concept is employed by requiring the stimulus strength to be in excess of $1.0 - P$ (partisanship). Therefore, if an individual has a Democratic "P" value of .6, then the stimulus strength must be greater than $1.0 - .6$, or .4, for him to choose the Democratic candidate as his initial preference.

This calculation, $1.0 - P$, also has another interpretation. Of course, 1.0 would be equivalent to the sum of all probabilities of voting for the various parties in the system plus the probability of abstention. Therefore, the subtraction of the partisanship value of a certain party from 1.0 yields a remainder, which could represent an index of "indifference" toward that

---

[24] McPhee and Smith, "A Model for Analyzing Voting Systems," p. 133.

given party. Consequently, for the voter to select that party as his initial choice, the stimulus strength generated by the above-cited Monte Carlo method must be greater than his "indifference" (1.0 − P) toward that party. To illustrate this point, suppose a voter had a .5 probability of voting for the Democratic nominee. His indifference toward the Democratic candidate would be 1.0 − .5, which equals .5. Therefore, a stimulus intensity greater than .5 would be sufficient reason for the voter to select the Democrat as his initial preference.

Furthermore, McPhee and his colleagues note the *extent* to which the stimulus exceeds the "indifference" level. In other words, it makes a difference in the previous example if the stimulus strength is 6, 7, or 8, etc. All values above 5 would yield a Democratic preference. However, the magnitude of the remainder of "stimulus"-"indifference" is employed as the *degree of interest* in one's choice. Thus, if the randomly generated stimulus were 7, "interest" would be equivalent to .7 − .5 ("stimulus strength" − "indifference"), or .2. The "interest" measure is employed during the discussion process as a basis for determining whether or not two people are sufficiently interested in the campaign to actually discuss the issues and to attempt to influence one another.

In addition, this fundamental relationship between stimulus and indifference has a direct bearing upon the overall election, since as partisanship increases, less stimulation is needed for a person to cross the interest threshold and thereby make the "choice." Furthermore, high stimulus campaigns are going to "activate" those who are less partisan. With weak partisan stimulation, only the party diehards will maintain their loyalty.

In sum, every individual has an "interest" measure for *each party*. More often than not, one "interest" index is positive, while the others are negative. In a two-party system, however, it is quite possible for a voter to receive high stimulus from both parties, thereby producing a positive interest in each party. In this case, the individual selects the party in which he is *more* interested.

After only the first stage of stimulation, this choice is interpreted as only a first impression or intention. Later, after other processes of the model that may or may not change it, the surviving choice, when "election day" comes is recorded as the final *decision* or conviction. . . . If no choice survives on election day, it means nonvoting. Interest in this no-choice situation—where the best stimulus-disposition combination does not reach the minimum—is the deficit below that indifference point, recorded without sign.[25]

Equipped with an initial choice (or non-choice) and a degree of interest, the individual is now ready to enter into discussion with members of his *primary* groups. During this interaction stage, two people may or may not exchange views on the election. The two people are referred to as "Ego" and "Alter," where "Ego" is the initiator of influence and "Alter" is the recipient of any influence. The voter in the model will be an "Ego" for one person while he will be the "Alter" for yet another voter. The statuses of "Ego" and "Alter" determine *which* individual during interaction will *initiate* or *receive* influence. The sociometric relationships in the simulation must be inferred by the researcher.

The process can be readily understood by consulting the revised flow chart in Figure 3.4. First "Ego" proceeds through the stimulation process and then enters the discussion process. At this point, his "Alter" is retrieved from storage and interaction ensues.

Discussion between "Ego" and "Alter" is contingent upon the level of "interest," as calculated during the stimulation process. If neither voter is very interested, they may forgo discussion altogether. Adequate interest, however, would prompt both individuals to mutually examine the election campaign. To put it in the terms of our model, "Ego" and "Alter" enter discussion if the *average interest (regardless of partisan direction) for both of them is greater than the indifference point.*

Any interchange of ideas would initially have the effect of informing the voter of the prevailing partisan position of his discussion partner.

As the flow chart indicates, disagreement causes both "Ego"

[25] *Ibid.*, pp. 138–39.

and "Alter" to return to the stimulation process, where absorption of additional stimuli may or may not generate new choices. Following this step, both return to storage, from whence they may return at a later date. If an individual does not return from storage to the discussion process before "election day," he will simply cast his vote in accordance with his present disposition.

Figure 3.4

Flow Diagram of Two People Going Through
McPhee's Socio-Psychological Model

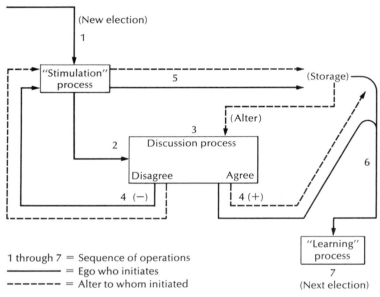

1 through 7 = Sequence of operations
————— = Ego who initiates
------- = Alter to whom initiated

Source: William N. McPhee and Robert B. Smith, "A Model for Analyzing Voting Systems," p. 129.

If the discussants mutually agree in their selection of a candidate, then "Alter" returns to storage and "Ego" "learns" his original choice.

> The socially supported choice, then, is not subjected to the possibly upsetting process of new stimulation. And thus supported, the choice will tend to survive to become the decision

as of election day. In mature stages of problem runs, sociometric cliques tend toward homogeneity and the voter is likely to be agreed with all along and thus his initial preference survives until election day unchanged.[26]

The individual, therefore, utilizes the discussion process as a means of finding social validation of tentative partisan choices. Consequently, primary group interaction would be crucial in facilitating stability or change in electoral patterns. *If the voter finds support for his initial choice, he discontinues interaction and retains this preference on election day. If his friends and associates don't agree with him, he exposes himself to more stimuli, thereby increasing the likelihood that he will change in the direction of his colleagues. This is the essence of social influence as implied by this socio-psychological simulation model.* "So, if we interpret the process as reinforcement theory, social intimates are the agents selecting *what* is to be reinforced and learned." [27]

However, disagreement does not lead to punitive action, since politics is generally not a central interest to the group. Instead, the decision is held in "abeyance."

At any rate, primary group influence in the discussion stage of the model has the greatest impact on people with weak predispositions. Those with low levels of partisanship are also more likely to be influenced upon restimulation. Conversely, strong party identifiers are going to be difficult to change either at the stimulation stage or during the discussion process. Therefore, influence is most likely to flow from highly partisan to less partisan voters.[28]

The last process of the model assumes that the present election will have an impact on the individual that will carry over to subsequent elections. After the election, the voter, having re-

[26] *Ibid.,* p. 147.

[27] *Ibid.,* p. 147.

[28] Observations on "opinion leadership" are consistent with this interpretation of influence. "Opinion leaders" tend to be more partisan, more politically involved, and better informed. These factors give the "opinion leader" an edge in an interpersonal interaction. See Berelson, Lazarsfeld, and McPhee, *Voting,* p. 117.

corded his "choice" at the polls, "learns" from his recent experience. "Learning," in this instance, means that the individual's partisanship will be modified by the vote he cast in the election just completed.

As previously stated, the "P" value is simply the proportion of times an individual voted for a party. These percentages are recalculated after adding in the vote of the present election. Computing partisanship indices in this manner

> . . . implies a substantive commitment, among many others, to an interpretation that the less cumulative experience (for example, the younger voter), the more influence any new experience will have in changing dispositions (changing P, partisanship). This result, of course, is just what we want in the case of voting, judging by all research evidence.[29]

The long-term effect of this phenomenon would be to

> . . . increase the chances in future elections of making the choices that survive discussion and perhaps reconsideration in the current election.[30]

"Choices" made in the next election are more likely to survive discussion if there are both a stronger stand in the interaction stage *and* the need for a smaller amount of consistent partisan appeal during the stimulation process. That the model makes provision for strong partisan values being maintained despite disparate partisan stimulation is consistent with Berelson, Lazarsfeld, and McPhee's observation that

> Partisans tend to perceive the candidate's stand on the issue as favorable to their own stand. (1) They perceive their candidate's stand as similar to their own and the opponent's stand as dissimilar. (2) They tend *not* to perceive differences with their own candidate or similarities to the opposition candidate.
>
> Voters who feel strongly about their choice are more likely

---

[29] McPhee and Smith, "A Model for Analyzing Voting Systems," p. 141.

[30] *Ibid.,* p. 141.

to misperceive the candidate's stands on the issues as favorable to their own positions.[31]

It would be presumptuous to assume that every election has equal weight in modifying partisan attachment. Some elections may be of little significance in redefining a "P" value, while other contests may have an indelible effect. Therefore, the impact of a "choice" on partisanship values is *weighted in accordance with the level of "interest" in the campaign.*

Furthermore, there is a "forgetting" factor built into the learning process of the simulation model. Systematic diminution of the effects of past elections is accomplished by mathematically adjusting the weight each election has during the recalculation of a "P" value. After every contest, the relative frequency of votes weighted by interest is multiplied by some constant less than 1.0. Older elections, having been downwardly adjusted more than recent ones, would have less impact on current partisanship values. This procedure is designed to approximate the forgetting of older experiences.

The learning process complete, the citizen is returned to storage with redefined dispositions of partisanship and non-voting. He now awaits the dawn of a new election period.

The socio-psychological model described in the preceding passages has serious long-run historical implications for the distribution of rank-and-file partisan loyalties. To fundamentally realign voters, this model requires that

> Appeals must be *sustained* over a number of elections, for example, as Democratic stimuli were sustained in the New Deal-Fair Deal era, to accomplish significant switching. . . .[32]

Three dissimilar applications of this socio-psychological model illustrate its utility for voting analysis. The first concerns itself with one election, while the other uses of the model are directed toward behavior involving "generations" of voters for many elections.

---

[31] Berelson, Lazarsfeld, and McPhee, *Voting,* p. 233.
[32] McPhee and Smith, "A Model for Analyzing Voting Systems," p. 143.

One application of the interaction model above was a simulation experiment with the 1960 Wisconsin primary election, in which the combatants were John F. Kennedy, Hubert H. Humphrey, and Richard M. Nixon.[33] In this instance, the basic information was survey data made available by Elmo Roper, Inc. Unlike the model described above, this model employed attitudinal data for estimating partisanship values and stimulus intensity levels of various campaign appeals made by the three candidates. Partisan disposition for each party or candidate was measured fairly easily using standard scaling techniques.

> The stimulus arrays F(s) are the real problem. One each is needed for each appeal as it bears on each candidate within each homogeneous demographic group, of which twenty groups were used in stratifying Wisconsin. The best raw data from which to postulate the form of such a stimulus distribution to input to any such group in the model are the dispersions of answers obtained when *real* members of the corresponding group in the prior survey were asked to rate how each such appeal struck them as an argument for the given cause, on scales graded from "strong argument" to "weak argument." . . .[34]

Since the Wisconsin primary is open, the primary could be considered a three-way contest insofar as voters could freely cross party lines. Since Nixon was unchallenged by any other Republican hopeful, one might expect that many Republicans would cross over to participate in the more crucial Democratic primary.

This application of the model is a most interesting example of how simulation can be a useful tool in "experimenting" with voting behavior. McPhee addressed his research to the possibility of Humphrey's improving his electoral performance by heating up the campaign. If the Minnesota Senator's "strongest" ap-

---

[33] See McPhee, *Public Opinion Quarterly*, Vol. XXV, No. 2 (Summer 1961), pp. 184–93.
[34] *Ibid.*, pp. 184–93.

peal, the farm issue, were intensified, and if Nixon's strength among voters were diminished, presumably Humphrey would pick up many Republican votes. In fact, under these conditions, Humphrey did receive support from Republican farmers. However, even in this experiment, he did not win the election. Balancing out his gains in electoral strength was the simultaneous cross-over of Catholic Republicans to the Kennedy camp. Furthermore, many middle-class, rural, Protestant Republicans, even when not strongly pro-Nixon, were not attracted to Humphrey, since the farm issue was not directly relevant to their own interests.

> The net result of the problem was that the weakening of the less numerous Republican Catholics for Kennedy almost exactly matched a (lower) proportion of the more numerous Protestant groups to Humphrey. So, even though the total crossing over of party lines in the final weeks was perhaps 25 to 30 percent of the original Nixon vote—at least 10 to 12 percent of the total—it left the statewide ratio between Kennedy and Humphrey almost exactly the same. Judging from the survey, there was also little net change in that ratio in Wisconsin. Thus, "dynamics" netted nothing, a result which is, if disappointing, realistic.[35]

The second major usage of the model involved an experiment with political immunization.[36] It was noted that when strong stimuli are broadcast to various segments of the public, sizable commitments to political parties are created. Therefore, it was hypothesized that voters in future elections would be resistant to changes—they would be "immunized" by constant reinforcement of their partisan attachments.

To experiment with this notion, the authors produced a hypothetical electorate of young voters, who had very little political experience, and who were not strongly committed to one side or the other.

Two political parties were operative in this system—the "dy-

---

[35] *Ibid.,* p. 193.
[36] McPhee and Ferguson, "Political Immunization," pp. 155–79.

namic" party and the "opposition" party. The partisan appeals of the "dynamic" party transmitted strong stimuli early in a "decade" of "elections," and later won control of the government. The level of stimulation declined back to normal, and the "dynamic" party lost power, thereby ending up right where it had started. The "opposition" party, however, provided a constant stimulus intensity, which tended to be biased toward some groups more than others.

This experimental design was intended to approximate conditions as they existed in such periods as the 1930s and the 1940s. It was hypothesized that during the second decade of computer "elections," individuals, having been conditioned by the first decade of participation, would have built up a resistance to change in voting habits. Subjecting this hypothesis to the computer model, the researchers found that

> . . . (1) there is an immunization effect in the model, a "damping" of the oscillatory swings in response to the same stimuli in successive decades, as would be expected of the model's theory . . . but, (2) The degree of such damping of response is *small* in any one decade's time (or *slow* as we consider many decades). The latter results had not been expected of the intuitive theory and are contrary to the impression given by voting research, namely, that party loyalties rapidly "rigidify" with maturity. If they do not rigidify quickly, however, and the effect of previous experience in damping out new responsiveness is no more than roughly that above, in the real American circumstances today, then the immunization effect would be of only academic interest, and insufficient for any real protection.[37]

McPhee and Ferguson argue that this computer result corresponds very well with the actual shifting electoral patterns of the New Deal era. Presenting Gallup data in support of their position, the authors demonstrate that although young voters provided strong backing for Franklin D. Roosevelt in 1936, they nevertheless abandoned him at a much greater rate than older voters when the Roosevelt appeal declined, and when

[37] *Ibid.,* pp. 159–60.

Wendell Willkie came to prominence in 1940. This conclusion is generally consistent with the observed phenomenon of greater oscillation among younger voters. Furthermore, by examining the Roosevelt, Truman, and Eisenhower eras, the writers conclude that, in spite of immunization effects, there are significant shifts in voting patterns across all age groups; and interestingly enough, the *direction* of the shift is usually *consistent for all age groups.*

The magnitude of oscillation in voting patterns, which occurs regardless of "damping" effects, has been documented by other scholarly political observers.

> Shifting voters are more numerous than is commonly supposed. Election returns subtly but erroneously suggest that they are few in number. . . .
>
> The switchers at individual elections over the period 1940–1960 probably ranged in number from about one eighth to about one fifth, or slightly more, of the survivors from those who had voted at the preceding election.[38]

Nevertheless, there are two reasons to suspect an immunization effect. In the first place, people who maintain a strong party identification are not very susceptible to disturbing propaganda. However, the "young" voters in the model are in moderate positions and are, therefore, quite receptive to strong stimuli. The intense stimulation that these inexperienced voters would receive has the effect of creating strong partisan attachments, which are not likely to be changed.

Secondly, interaction among primary group members would have the effect of reinforcing partisan commitments. The group provides a social context that facilitates political discussion, which, in turn, leads to reinforcement of a generally held position within the group. When the direction of group partisanship is congruent with the strong stimuli transmitted by the "dynamic" party, political immunization ensues. In addition, when the appeals are altered during the second "decade" of elections,

---

[38] V. O. Key, Jr., *The Responsible Electorate* (New York: Vintage Books, 1968), pp. 16–17.

the impact of the group is such that the predispositions of the individual members remain relatively stable, even in the face of strong appeals by the "opposition" party. The long-run consequences of this phenomenon would be that

> . . . the new hero or demagogue faces not just the problem of converting the individuals, but groups: to keep that individual persuaded, *simultaneously* converting his family, friends, and group leadership.[39]

Although these two factors are at work in the model, the simulation reveals an attending lack of effective political immunization, which is attributable to two disturbances in the process.

First of all, a great number of people are not committed to any one party. The shifts are not among people attached to either the "dynamic" or "opposition" party, but are among those who wouldn't vote at all unless strongly stimulated.

> That is, the exchanges that keep the system from damping out are between the "Dynamic" party and a pool of marginally *indifferent* people who, not cultivated by the "Opposition" and only voting for the "Dynamic" party's heroes in their heroic period, never become permanently committed. Being noncommitted they remain a pool of potential votes for the next hero, wherever he comes from. And this pool remains large enough again to destroy the balance between the committed partisans who, without these marginal people, would hold each other in check after the first decade or so. It is not, then, that the involved persons fail to be immunized against *each other;* it is that neither is protected against a *third group* where, so to speak, the initial vaccinating experience "didn't take." [40]

Secondly, there is simply not enough consensus, or one-sidedness, within groups. Consequently, reinforcement by interaction within primary groups does not proceed at the rate one might expect.

---

[39] McPhee and Ferguson, "Political Immunization," p. 171.
[40] *Ibid.,* p. 172.

Two variants of this original model were run in order to demonstrate the immunizing effects of slightly intensified political activity. One version provided stronger stimuli to individuals on behalf of both parties ("dynamic" and "opposition"), while the other modification had more biased (not stronger) appeals to groups. Both variants of the simulation model produced substantial damping out of oscillation in electoral patterns.

The sizable immunizing effects accruing from slight increases in stimulation and bias indicate that it might be theoretically possible to have stimuli strong enough to commit everybody, and a high degree of group-anchored partisanship which would reinforce the attachments of individual members.

> Strangely, this extremity would produce a perfect moderation in the system, a total electorate that would move gently and never stray far from 50-50. But that "system moderation" would require quarreling so intense as to make all its *individual* parts grotesquely immoderate, blindly partisan individuals and one-sided groups.[41]

Finally, the third application of the model involved a simulated exercise in political socialization.[42] In this case, the interaction pair during the discussion process was a "parent" and his "child." Both of these discussion partners could receive various levels of partisan stimuli. The basic concern in this instance was to explore the nature of parental influence on the individual's voting behavior. Nine "elections," spread over two "decades," were used. At the outset, the new voters were assigned relatively low "P" values.

The results indicated the existence of differential socialization effects. For those young voters not interacting with a "parent," there was no noticeable increase in partisanship toward the "parent's" party. However, young voters interacting with a "parent" generally showed a substantial increase in their attach-

41 *Ibid.*, p. 179.
42 Ferguson and Smith, "A Theory of Informal Social Influence," pp. 74–79.

ment to the parental party. In fact, when interaction was discontinued during the second "decade," the young voters still voted for the parental party because they had internalized the adult predispositions.

Examination of the election outcomes after different levels of stimulation is quite revealing. Those young voters who received strong partisan stimuli voted for the "dynamic" party regardless of whether or not it simultaneously represented the choice of the parent. The parental influence led to only minor attrition when the "child's" initial preference was not the same as the parent's choice. However, when a young voter was not consistent with his parent *and,* at the same time, was exposed to *low* stimulation from his own party, he was much more likely to abandon his original preference. The logical conclusion is that constant, strong stimulation would be needed to generate fundamental deviations from the parental position.

In addition, it was found that the children's voting behavior oscillated over several elections if the strength of the stimulation of the "opposition" party oscillated. A finding, which is not as intuitively obvious, is the discovery of a condition under which the children's vote choice varies even if his party's stimulus intensity remains constant over the years. This occurs when the parent's party, even though the opposite of the child's preference, transmits oscillating stimuli, which leads to differential "interest" in the campaign. The varying degree of interest, in turn, partly determines the social influence of the parent during the discussion process. In other words, increased parental interest means that there is a greater likelihood that the disagreeing "child" will be exposed to disturbing stimuli, which may alter his existing preference.

It was concluded that the parent's ability to change the child's voting behavior was greatest if the parent initiated influence when the child's party was providing oscillating stimuli, as is often the case during the period of declining appeal of the "dynamic" party. Therefore, greatest Democratic Party inroads could have been made during the mid-1950s, if the parent were interested in overcoming Republican control.

These three specific applications of the "socio-psychological" simulations illustrate that the work of McPhee *et al.* is the most imaginative use of primary group interaction theory as it relates to voting behavior. Both short-term (e.g. the Wisconsin primary election) and long-term (e.g. "generations" of voters) analyses provide unique perspectives on voter decision-making. In the future, this socio-psychological model may require more emphasis on the *content,* as well as the intensity, of stimulation, and on experimenting with complex types of interaction.

The Individual Level of Analysis:
Two Theoretical Models of Voter Decision-Making

The remainder of this chapter will be devoted to the description of two theoretical models which focus almost exclusively upon individual behavior. Unlike the Simulmatics models and McPhee's simulations, neither the Downsian rational actor model nor the Survey Research Center's six-component model has been tested by computer simulation. Therefore, these two models will be expressed in flow diagrams which can be readily translated into computer programming language.

THE DOWNSIAN RATIONAL VOTER

Recognizing the importance of group membership and primary group interaction, Anthony Downs nevertheless opts for a more purely individual level of analysis.[43] The Downsian voter is a "rational actor" by virtue of his ability to employ his vote as a means of accomplishing political or economic ends. This rational voter seeks to maximize his benefits, which in this model, include ". . . streams of utility from government activity." The citizen may utilize government services ranging from welfare payments and highways to police protection and recreation facilities. Furthermore, Downs argues that the individual may receive benefit from action that may not directly enhance his material well-being. To the contrary,

> There can be no simple identification of "acting for one's own greatest benefit" with selfishness in the narrow sense because self-denying charity is often a great source of benefits to one-

[43] Anthony Downs, *An Economic Theory of Democracy,* p. 8.

self. Thus our model leaves room for altruism in spite of its basic reliance upon the self-interest axiom.[44]

It is on the basis of utility income that the voter determines whether he will support the party controlling the government apparatus or the party currently out of power. However, since a citizen can unknowingly receive benefits from government, one must introduce a constraint on the individual's calculus—i.e. the voter can only consider *perceived* utility income.

Perceived utility is the fundamental element required to compute an "expected party differential":

$$EPD = E(U^A t + 1) - E(U^B t + 1)$$

where

EPD = expected party differential
E = expected value
U = utility income
A = incumbent party
t = present election period
$t + 1$ = next election period
B = opposition party.

The EPD is simply the degree to which an individual would expect greater utility income if one party were in power rather than another. A positive EPD would dictate a vote for the incumbent (party A), while a negative EPD would lead the rational actor to cast his ballot for the opposition (party B). An expected party differential of zero would mean that the potential voter saw no political or economic grounds for selecting either party. Consequently, he would have no rational option other than abstention.

The reader, no doubt, is aware that expectations about the future behavior of political parties may never be fully realized since parties do not (or cannot) always deliver on campaign promises. Downs suggests, therefore, that the voter must attempt to visualize utility flows as they might exist if each party were actually in power during election period $t + 1$. The actions

[44] *Ibid.*, p. 27.

of the party already in power (party A) do provide some insight as to what it may do in future election periods. Nevertheless, as Downs rightfully points out, comparing a present utility flow generated by the party in power with expected future utility income from the opposition is invalid, since these indices constitute evaluations of two different election periods (t and t + 1). A solution is available to the voter if he estimates the utility income he would have received had the opposition been in power during election period t.

> True, this performance is purely hypothetical; so he can only imagine what utility he would have derived from it. But party B's future is hypothetical, too—as is that of party A. Thus he must either compare (1) two hypothetical future incomes or (2) one actual present utility income and one hypothetical present one. Without question, the latter comparison allows him to make more direct use of concrete facts than the former. Not only is one of its terms a real entity, but the other can be calculated in full view of the situation from which it springs. If he compares future utility incomes, he enjoys neither of these advantages. Therefore, we believe it is more rational for him to ground his voting decision on current events than purely future ones.[45]

Therefore, the voter calculates the "major determinant of his expected party differential"—his "current party differential."

$$CPD = (U^A t) - E(U^B t)$$

where

  $CPD =$ current party differential
  $U^A t =$ utility actually received while party A was in power during election period t
  $E(U^B t) =$ hypothetical utility income had party B been in power during election period t.

However, in order to assure that his decision will be attuned to the election period t + 1, the rational actor employs two "future-orienting" modifiers.

The first modifier is a "trend factor," which is

[45] *Ibid.*, p. 40.

> . . . the adjustment each citizen makes in his current party differential to account for any relevant trend in events that occurs within the current election period.[46]

To illustrate how the individual makes use of this factor, consider a situation in which the party in power began election period t by not providing a sufficient flow of utility for the voter. As time passed, however, the controlling party became able to provide the desired benefits. Taking into account such progress, the rational voter may decide to lend his electoral support to the incumbents. On the other hand, of course, the "trend" of the incumbent party's governing prowess may be negative, and therefore detrimental to the voter's utility income. If enough citizens perceive such an unfavorable trend, the party in power may very well become the opposition party in election period t + 1.

The second "future-orienting" factor Downs labels a "performance rating."

> The second modifier comes in to play *only* when the citizen cannot see any difference between the two parties running; i.e. when he thinks they have identical platforms and current policies. To escape from this deadlock, he alters the basis of his decision to whether or not the incumbents have done as good a job of governing as did their predecessors in office.[47]

This factor may be used on certain occasions when the individual has a zero party differential, which can be caused by one of two things:

1. The political parties have identical policies and platforms. Consequently, the expected utility income is equal for both parties.

2. The parties are expected to provide the same utility income, in spite of the fact that their policies and platforms show a marked difference.

> In the latter case, performance ratings are useless to him because he already knows what changes will take place if the op-

---

[46] *Ibid.*, p. 41.
[47] *Ibid.*, p. 41. My italics.

position wins. Since these changes do not alter his utility income, he abstains. But in the former case he does not know what changes the opposition will make; hence he needs some way to determine his attitude toward change in general.[48]

Therefore, the performance rating, which reflects the extent to which the individual believes the governing party is doing a good job of providing governmental services, comes into play when the parties have identical policies and platforms. Of course, the criterion of good performance is defined by the individual himself.

With the incorporation of these two "future-orienting factors," the basic calculation is redefined. The voter modifies the original estimate of his "current party differential" in accordance with the perceived importance of the trend factor. Those who perceive identical policies alter their zero party differentials by the use of performance ratings. However, the individual still votes for the incumbent if his modified CPD is positive he votes for the opposition if it is negative, and abstains if it is zero.

For those citizens who have either a positive or negative differential, there is still another fundamental computation to be made. The individual knows that his vote is unlikely to have a decisive impact on the final election outcome because of the large number of people voting. Consequently, the importance of any one vote varies in accordance with the closeness of the election. If the margin of victory is substantial, a single vote is almost insignificant. A very close election, however, increases the relative importance of a single vote, since only a handful of votes may determine the ultimate outcome. Downs argues that the individual "discounts" his party differential on the basis of the expected closeness of the election. If the voter believes the election will be one-sided, then the importance of voting declines (i.e. the party differential is greatly "discounted"). In an election which is perceived to be close, the voter does not "discount" his party differential nearly so much. The discounted party differential is referred to as the "vote value."

[48] *Ibid.*, p. 44.

This vote value is compounded from his estimates of his party differential and of the probability that his vote will be decisive. Since the vote value measures the possible cost to him of being adequately informed, it is from the vote value, not the party differential, that information relevant to voting derives its worth.[49]

Up to this point, the discussion has been concerned primarily with *benefits* to be received, with very little attention being paid to the *costs* which may be incurred. Of course, many costs may be associated with electoral participation. Nevertheless, Downs directs a major share of his effort toward delineating the role of "information costs" in the voter's calculations.

There are many different types of costs connected with the use of information. On the one hand, there are procurement, analysis, and evaluation costs, and on the other hand, there are assimilation costs. The first three are labeled by Downs as "transferable" costs, while the last one is a "non-transferable" cost, since every voter must, at the very minimum, assimilate information.

The transferable costs (procurement, analysis, and evaluation) can be greatly diminished by having others, such as television news commentators or newspapermen, collect, analyze, and evaluate information relevant to governmental operations. Many of the news media are in a position to initiate such a vast undertaking, whereas the individual would be physically, mentally, and financially incapable of handling this chore. Since the gathering of data alone is such an enormous task, the voter often attempts to "transfer" the burden of procuring, analyzing, and evaluating information.

In order not to be propagandized by those of opposing views, the citizen samples the analytical and evaluative approaches of many reporters to various political and governmental problems. He then transfers information costs to the agency which employs his own means of selecting, analyzing, and evaluating information. Occasionally, the voter reviews other media to assure himself that the "reporter" he has chosen is still consistent with his own preferences.

[49] *Ibid.*, pp. 244–45.

Information costs may be further reduced with the acquisition of "accidental" data.

> Accidental data are by-products of the non-political activities of a citizen; they accrue to him without any special effort on his part to find them.[50]

"Sought-for" data, such as documents published by interest groups, although "free" political information in one sense usually imply a greater cost to the recipient, since a conscious effort is made to collect documents and assimilate their contents. "Accidental" data, however, cost very little owing to the fact that the individual does not expend a great deal of effort in procuring them.

The rational voter's use of political data needs some clarification. In the first place, information costs are largely ignored when forming initial estimates of the party differential. Additional information is collected only if it is expected to modify the original party differential. Therefore, the process of estimation proceeds in the following manner:

> The first step in estimation of one's party differential, either (1) by means of the free information which one absorbs in daily living, or (2) by means of data obtained in an exploratory investment made just for this purpose.
> The preliminary estimate of the party differential is the basic return upon which subsequent calculations are built. It is the estimated cost of being wrong, derived without serious consideration of the cost and returns of making the estimate. *From this point on, however, the costs and returns of all data must be weighed and information procured only if its expected return exceeds its cost.*[51]

Since additional information is collected only if it is expected to change one's present position, then it follows that those citizens with the strongest candidate preferences will probably not seek any new data. It is also a logical extension of this principle that people with zero party differentials will probably not

---

[50] *Ibid.*, p. 223.
[51] *Ibid.*, p. 241. My italics.

procure information, since the data would have to lead to the inference that the apathetic individual's utility income would be significantly affected by one party or another having control of the governmental apparatus. Of the indifferent person, it can be said that

> . . . unless new data reveal a very large change in some expected income, it does not really make much difference to him who wins. Therefore, it is irrational for him to acquire many costly bits unless they have either large expected values or high variance relative to his original party differential. Only such data can raise his party differential so that he is no longer indifferent about voting correctly.[52]

If, in the final analysis, perceived *benefits* of voting for one party outweigh the *costs* incurred during the process of deliberation, then the person casts his ballot for the party of his choice.

However, Downs points out that the utility income returns from voting are often negligible for most citizens. Consequently, even rather minor costs can outweigh benefits. However, rational citizens still vote because, in addition to any impact upon utility income, voting has value in and of itself. Benefits accrue to an individual merely by living in a democracy, and maintenance of a democratic society relies heavily upon the electoral participation of the citizenry. Therefore, rational men experience a sense of social responsibility to vote. This responsibility, in turn, leads to benefits stemming from the continuation of democratic processes. Consequently, voting has value *per se,* as well as value in extracting benefits from government.

> Although the benefits each citizen derives from living in a democracy actually accrue to him continuously over time, he can view them as a capital sum which pays interest at each election. This procedure is rational because voting is a necessary prerequisite for democracy; hence democracy is in one sense a

---

[52] *Ibid.,* p. 243.

reward for voting. We call the part of this reward the citizen receives at each election his *long-run participation value*.[53]

The various elements discussed thus far—party differential, future-orienting modifiers, discounted party differential, long-run participation value, and voting costs—are all brought together in a model which weighs benefits against costs. Where benefits outweigh costs, the citizen votes in accordance with his preferences; otherwise he abstains.

The structure of the overall process model is reflected in the flow diagram in Figure 3.5. After making initial estimates of his party differential, voting costs, long-run participation value, and the number of people he believes will vote, the rational actor contemplates the direction of his party differential and his estimate of the closeness of the election. Let us assume that he calculates a pro-Republican party differential. If his discounted party differential plus his long-run participation value exceed his voting costs, he votes Republican. A net value of zero or less prompts the citizen to abstain. The same procedure is employed if his party differential is pro-Democratic. Of course, a net positive value would produce a Democratic vote.

With a zero party differential the voter must determine whether he perceives the same policies or platforms in both parties. If he perceives policy differences, his utility income is unaffected by either party's platform. Consequently, the only return he gets from the election is his long-run participation value. If his long-run participation value is greater than his voting costs, the individual votes randomly, since he has no other rational basis for selection. If voting costs are too great, the rational citizen abstains.

If the person with a zero party differential perceives the same policies or platforms in both parties, he then alters his basis of decisions to performance ratings. If the expected value of "change" or "no change," in combination with the person's long-run participation value, is greater than the cost of voting, he votes. If the resulting value is zero or less, the citizen abstains. If the benefits outweigh costs and "no change" is pre-

[53] *Ibid.*, p. 270. Downs's italics.

FIGURE 3.5
FLOW DIAGRAM OF DOWNSIAN DECISION-MAKING MODEL

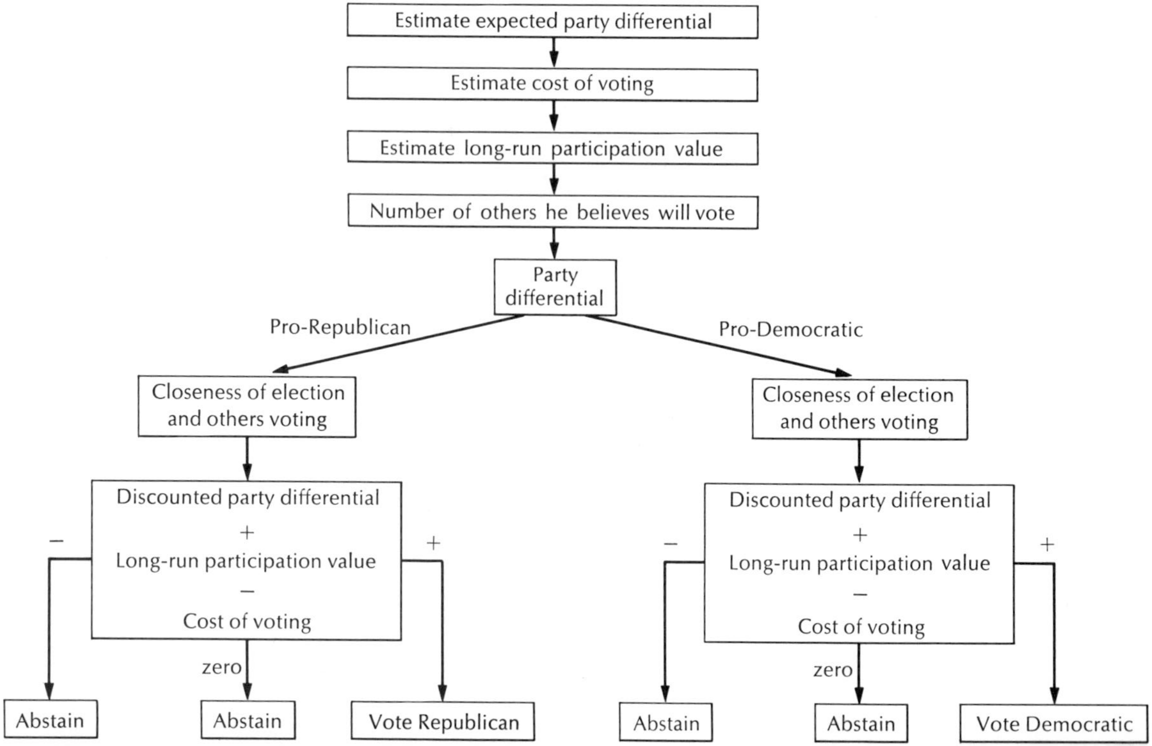

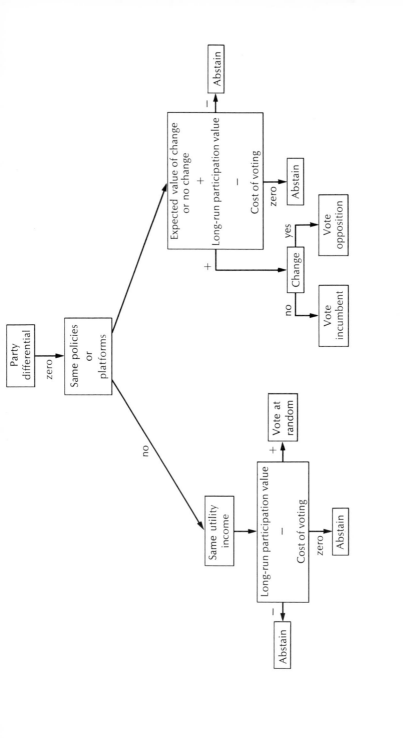

ferred, the voter casts his ballot for the incumbent. If "change" is preferred, the rational voter supports the opposition party.

As indicated in Chapter Two, a flow diagram forms the basis of a process model. The model depicted in Figure 3.5 will first be precisely expressed in a computer program; then it will be tested with survey data. In addition, various parameters of the model will be subjected to sensitivity testing, and a Downsian interpretation of the election under study will be presented.

Two modifications of this general model will also be tested by computer simulation. In one version of the model, party identification will be introduced into the decision-making process. Party loyalty can play a role in the Downsian rational calculus, since

> . . . some rational men habitually vote for the same party in every election. In several preceding elections, they carefully informed themselves about all the competing parties, and all the issues of the moment; yet they always came to the same decision about how to vote. Therefore, they have resolved to repeat this decision automatically without becoming well-informed, unless some catastrophe makes them realize it no longer expresses their best interests. Like all habits, this one saves resources, since it keeps voters from investing in information which would not alter their behavior. Thus it is a rational habit. Habitual voters are either *loyalists,* who always vote for the same party, or *apathetics,* who always abstain because they believe their party differentials are forever zero.[54]

Those who have a *zero party differential* will be tested for party identification, which can be rationally employed in *place of party differential.* If no party identification is prevalent, the voter will proceed with the usual calculations relating to zero party differentials. This computer simulation should indicate the relative importance of partisan attachment in the overall process.

The second modification involves the use of ideology as a decision-making factor. In this instance, the voter examines party ideologies rather than specific issues.

[54] *Ibid.,* p. 85. Downs's italics.

> Such behavior is rational in two situations (1) having informed himself reasonably well, the voter cannot distinguish between parties on an issue basis, but can on an ideology basis; or (2) he votes by means of ideologies in order to save himself the cost of becoming informed about specific issues. In both cases . . . he uses an *ideology differential* to make his decision, since he is without sufficient data to formulate a nonzero party differential.[55]

Ideology will be incorporated into the model in the same manner as party identification. Those with zero party differentials will attempt to differentiate between the parties on the basis of ideological stance. Presumably this simulation will test the weight attached to ideological considerations in the voter's decision-making process.

SURVEY RESEARCH CENTER SIX-COMPONENT MODEL

The second model to be tested by way of computer simulation is the University of Michigan Survey Research Center's six-component model.[56] In this instance, an attempt has been made to construct a model which incorporates that set of attitudinal factors which bears on individual choice in any given election. In other words, both long-term and short-term forces need to be captured in a theoretical statement of the voter decision-making process. This model also expresses voting behavior at the individual level of analysis and recognizes the long-term effect of such factors as party identification. However,

> It is quite clear that fixed party loyalties and sociological characteristics cannot account fully for the vote. In particular, neither of these factors, relatively inert through time, can account

---

[55] *Ibid.,* p. 99. Downs's italics.

[56] See Donald E. Stokes, Angus Campbell, and Warren E. Miller, "Components of Electoral Decision," *The American Political Science Review,* Vol. LII, No. 2 (June 1958), pp. 367–87; and Donald E. Stokes, "Some Dynamic Elements of Contests for the Presidency," *The American Political Science Review,* Vol. LX, No. 1 (March 1966), pp. 19–28.

for the short-term fluctuations in the division of the vote which are of great significance in a two-party system.[57]

It has been argued that a model which takes into account both long-term and short-term forces for any given election necessarily considers an individual's position on the following dimensions:

> . . . (1) attitude toward the Democratic candidate as a person; (2) attitude toward the Republican candidate as a person; (3) attitude toward the parties and candidates which relates to the benefit of various groups; (4) attitude toward the parties and candidates which relates to domestic policy; (5) attitude which relates to foreign policy; and (6) attitude which relates to the general performance of the parties in the nation's affairs.[58]

A series of open-ended questions is used to determine an individual's attitude on these six components. A maximum of five responses is recorded for both the favorable and unfavorable remarks about the parties and about the candidates. Each response is then classified as reflecting one of the six attitudinal components. The Survey Research Center has employed a very simple procedure to measure a person's attitudinal direction for any one of the six components.

> In scoring a person's attitude toward a given object we have merely subtracted the number of his pro-Republican or anti-Democratic references to the object from the number of his anti-Republican or pro-Democratic references.[59]

In the past these attitude scores have been defined as the independent variables in a multiple correlation analysis. The de-

---

[57] Donald E. Stokes, Angus Campbell, and Warren E. Miller, "Components of Electoral Decision," p. 368.

[58] Donald E. Stokes, "Some Dynamic Elements of Contests for the Presidency," p. 20.

[59] Donald E. Stokes, Angus Campbell, and Warren E. Miller, "Components of Electoral Decision," p. 370.

pendent variable has been the partisan choice.[60] The relative importance of any one independent variable has been assessed by adjusting the difference between the mean value of a component's scores and the theoretical zero point by the component's beta weight.[61] This value can become the basis for inferring the differential impact of the components in any given election, or it can be employed to analyze component trends over several elections. In addition, the multiple regression equation, with partisan choice as the dependent variable, has been used to predict aggregate outcomes, and to estimate the probability of an individual voting for one party or the other.

In the present study, the Survey Research Center's six-component model will be expressed in a computer simulation program. The use of this model in simulating the voter's decision-making process is a slight departure from previous applications. Instead of focusing upon correlation and regression analysis, which utilizes a dichotomous expression of partisan preference, the author will attempt to predict three categorical outcomes— voting Democratic, voting Republican, and abstaining. In addition, the impact of each component on the decision-making model will be inferred by sensitivity testing of all six parameters.

The flow diagram in Figure 3.6 summarizes the model. The net Democratic preference valences are summed for all six components. A positive value yields a Democratic vote prediction, a negative value leads to a Republican vote prediction, and a zero value predicts an abstention. It is assumed that abstainers reached their position because their attitudes toward the parties and candidates show no net favorability of one party or the other. In other words, abstaining, as well as voting Democratic or Republican, is a function of the individual's net position on these attitudinal components.

The present use of the SRC six-component model is an attempt to *predict the nature of the behavioral act of voting rather than the preferences of the voter.* Although the voting

---

[60] The multiple correlation over several elections has ranged between .70 and .75.

[61] Beta weight is the slope of a relationship of two or more variables.

Figure 3.6
Flow Diagram of Survey Research Center
Six-Component Model

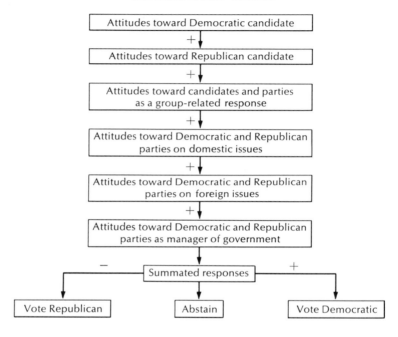

and preferences should be highly correlated, the attention is focused upon the act of voting.

Furthermore, by incorporating the predictive categories of Democratic vote, Republican vote, and abstain, the model will produce results which are comparable to the Downsian simulation outcomes. Consequently, in addition to *testing each model separately, it will be possible to undertake a comparative evaluation of the Downsian and SRC models.*

4 Measuring Downsian model parameters

The data employed to test both the Downsian and Survey Research Center models is the University of Michigan Survey Research Center 1964 presidential election study. One should be aware that testing any model on the basis of this, or any other, presidential election runs the risk of being inappropriate for two reasons: (1) presidential elections may be atypical of any other type of electoral contest, and (2) the 1964 presidential election may be unrepresentative of other presidential elections. In the former instance, the researcher would be unable to generalize from the 1964 contest to other kinds of elections. In the latter case, all conclusions would be unique to the 1964 presidential contest. Consequently, this writer will confine his remarks to the 1964 presidential election, and simply wait for others to replicate his work using other types of electoral contests. Unfortunately, this means that the findings of the present research undertaking may not be generalizable to other elections.

Yet another difficulty arises from the use of the SRC 1964 presidential election data—i.e. the measurement of the Downsian model parameters. No real problem occurs in testing the SRC six-component model, since the open-ended questions required to elicit responses on the six dimensions are included in the study. However, items were not constructed to measure the attitudes incorporated in the Downsian rational calculus. Consequently, indices must be constructed in order to estimate the parameters of the model.

Two such indices will be devised on an a priori basis. In the first place, the direction of an individual's party differential is determined by his response to the following question: "Do you think it will make any difference in how you and your family get along financially whether the Republicans or the Democrats win the election?" [1] If the respondent sees a financial advantage in having either party in office, he displays a differential toward that party. There can be no doubt that the criterion of family finance directly reflects utility income. Nevertheless, the Downsian concept of "streams of utility" from government operations encompasses a much wider range of benefits, unless one is prepared to argue that the rational actor interprets government activities as either adding to or detracting from his financial status. For present purposes, such an assumption is made. Even though the concept of "utility" may include any number of benefits, the present parameter estimate unquestionably taps attitudes relating to economic advantage, while at the same time conforming to the self-interest axiom basic to Downsian logic.

One other index, a measure of party identification, is constructed from one survey item:

> Generally speaking, do you usually think of yourself as a Republican, a Democrat, an Independent, or what? (If Republican or Democratic) Would you call yourself a strong (Republican) (Democrat) or not a very strong (Republican) (Democrat)? (If Independent or other) Do you think of yourself as closer to the Republican or Democratic party? [2]

This item has been traditionally employed as an indicator of partisan attachment, and in this research effort it will be used in the party identification modification of the Downsian model, which was discussed in the last chapter.

---

[1] Taken from the University of Michigan Survey Research Center 1964 presidential election study.
[2] *Ibid.*

Other Downsian concepts, such as information costs and long-run participation value, are not so clearly reflected in the SRC survey items. However, these dimensions of rational calculation may very well exist in the responses to a battery of survey items included in the 1964 study. Consequently, responses to thirty-five survey questions to components were factor analyzed in order to describe the underlying dimensions of attitude present in a wide range of response patterns. The thirty-five variables included in the factor analysis are presented in Appendix A.

Both party differential and party identification items are included in the analysis. However, the party differential represents only the *intensity* of the differential and not its *direction.*

The party identification item is coded such that the largest value is the strongest Republican identification and the smallest value is the strongest Democratic attachment.

Any responses to questions of public policy are recoded so that the individual's attitude is measured in relationship to his perception of the Republican and Democratic party positions. For example, if a person is in favor of school integration, and he believes that the Democrats will do more for school integration, he is coded a "3." If this person believes the Republican Party would do more, he is coded a "1." If he sees no difference between the parties, his score is "2." Alternatively, if an individual is against moves toward school integration, and thinks the Democrats will assist in school integration, he is coded pro-Republican ("1"). If he believes the Republicans will accelerate integration, he is coded as pro-Democratic ("3"). If he sees no difference in the parties' position, he is coded a "2." The attempt here is to express a respondent's attitude in terms of any perceived congruence between his own policy position and that of the two parties.

In addition, the response categories, although similar, are not exactly alike for all attitude items. For example, some items may have three response categories, while others may have five or six. However, all responses of uncertainty (e.g. "DK," "other," "NA") are assigned the middle value on our scale.

As previously indicated, these thirty-five variables became the input to a factor analysis routine. In order to more readily identify the underlying attitudinal dimensions, the original factor loadings were subjected to a mathematical technique which provides results that are easier to interpret. Application of this method, technically known as "varimax rotation," [3] to the thirty-five measures, resulted in a matrix of rotated factor loadings which are presented in Table 4.1. These rotated factor loadings represent the correlations of the individual survey items with the underlying factor. As is the case for simple product moment correlations, the factor loading has a range of -1.0 to $+1.0$. Also included in the table are the latent roots, and the cumulative percentage of the latent roots.[4] Finally, the communality (i.e., h^2, the variance in the item which is explained by all the factors combined) is presented for each variable. Note that ten underlying factors, each having a latent root greater than 1.0, were extracted from the original correlation matrix. Each of these factors will now be discussed.

FACTOR 1—INFORMATION COSTS

Employing a Downsian frame of reference, the first factor appears to reflect the information costs incurred by the voter. The extent to which the respondent made use of newspapers, radio, magazines, and television in order to gain information is critical to the naming of this factor. The item which contributes the

---

[3] The varimax criterion is one of the widely used techniques of rotation which offers an orthogonal solution—i.e. the factors remain uncorrelated after rotation has been achieved. Generally speaking, the varimax rotation criterion will maximize a variable's loading on one factor, and minimize its loadings on other factors. Consequently, interpretation of the dimensions inferred from a factor analysis is greatly simplified.

For a thorough discussion of varimax rotation and other factor analytic techniques, consult the following sources: Raymond Gernard Cattell, *Factor Analysis* (New York: Harper, 1952); Benjamin Fruchter, *Introduction to Factor Analysis* (New York: Van Nostrand, 1954); Harry Horace Harman, *Modern Factor Analysis* (New York: University of Chicago Press, 1960); Paul Horst, *Factor Analysis of Data Matrices* (New York: Holt, Rinehart and Winston, 1965); Donald F. Morrison, *Multivariate Statistical Methods* (New York: McGraw-Hill, 1967).

[4] Sometimes latent roots are referred to as "characteristic roots" or "eigenvalues." The latent root measures the amount of variation explained by the factor, while per cent of latent roots represents the percent of total variation accounted for by the factor.

most to a substantive interpretation of this dimension is the mass media usage index, which is simply the number of different media types utilized by the respondent. An appropriate name for this dimension is the "information cost" factor.

FACTOR 2—SENSE OF POLITICAL EFFICACY

It is most difficult to apply the language of the Downsian rational actor to this factor. The highest factor loadings appear on those items usually associated with a measure of a "sense of political efficacy." Furthermore, the moderate loading of income level on this factor is consistent with past findings.

FACTOR 3—INTENSITY OF PARTY DIFFERENTIAL

Factor 3 can best be interpreted as the intensity of the party differential in reverse. Both the intensity of the party differential (item 2) and the extent to which a person cares about the outcome of the election (item 34) load negatively on this dimension. Furthermore, it is quite reasonable that a general attentiveness to the campaign would also relate to a concern with the election outcome.

FACTOR 4—LONG-RUN PARTICIPATION VALUE

Downsian logic emphasizes that people receive benefits from living in a democracy, regardless of which party is in power. It is also self-evident that no democracy can function without elections. Therefore, the perceived value of participating in elections is contingent upon the individual's belief that elections perform the basic function of maintaining the linkage between the government and the people. This interpretation can be applied directly to factor 4.

In the first place, variable 16 most definitely taps the respondents' belief in the effectiveness of elections in forcing the government to pay attention to the people. Secondly, item 15 reflects the extent to which a person thinks the political party, the chief electoral apparatus for political recruitment, makes the government responsive to the people. Finally, the value of participating in elections is measured by the degree to which a person believes Congressmen pay attention to the people who *elect* them.

TABLE 4.1
ROTATED FACTOR LOADINGS—1964 SURVEY ITEMS
Factor

Variable	I	II	III	IV	V	VI
1	−.01843	−.01856	.01000	.03240	.19515	.09856
2	−.03096	−.04757	−.58956	−.01009	−.27988	.10716
3	.29844	.18936	−.60440	.07610	.20262	.07279
4	−.02751	.68749	−.10176	.11964	−.00752	−.05871
5	.16850	.53813	.20445	.01954	−.05511	.24659
6	.14415	.57830	−.24268	−.07013	.05253	.15681
7	.04362	.66097	−.09638	.26240	.03669	−.08271
8	.56275	.20164	−.26528	.05860	.24812	−.05907
9	.73172	−.14675	.05939	.02787	−.18513	.05797
10	.54154	.33697	−.07390	.08482	.18820	.23924
11	.45498	−.01665	−.25142	.06243	.07094	.18839
12	.91185	.16332	−.11755	.09137	.08550	.04095
13	.38208	.17676	−.52915	.20970	.24160	−.02682
14	.45138	.18509	−.33359	.16901	.31085	.17219
15	.03818	.07668	−.07877	.78408	−.02721	.03413
16	.08161	.10646	−.09734	.75756	.01306	−.01967
17	.08358	.12183	−.02700	.71938	−.01224	.07772
18	−.00206	−.04168	.03313	−.05854	.64884	−.08327
19	.14941	.03998	−.10219	.04117	−.01885	.29939
20	.14139	.22541	−.12399	.00280	.06579	.42879
21	−.03854	−.02183	−.15226	.02181	.11346	.55336
22	.04607	.00425	−.06479	.08087	−.09193	.58043
23	−.02929	.03980	.00814	−.03546	−.04076	.18288
24	.01369	−.01721	−.09806	.11994	.12957	.21482
25	.08994	.17206	.02150	−.00185	.02249	.08264
26	−.05674	.05345	−.14652	.06002	−.04728	.11535
27	−.02605	.04641	−.05518	.02141	−.01052	.13922
28	.04738	−.12135	.24782	−.12958	.35509	.26475
29	.11598	.11867	.25928	−.06681	.46186	.25012
30	.14044	.15777	−.14168	.04804	.55623	.09370
31	.28310	.09255	−.02000	−.05320	.26257	.17891
32	.26116	.03039	.04049	.04255	.22233	.12145
33	.13069	.01697	.00772	.04614	.05198	−.06509
34	.09327	.07475	−.63571	.11318	.02427	.15225
35	.07195	.47292	.08280	.14637	.28608	−.00726
Latent Root	2.89635	2.25611	2.04815	1.99420	1.78493	1.51970
Cumulative % of Latent Roots	.08275	.14721	.20573	.26271	.31371	.35713

Note: The highest factor loading for each variable has been underlined. This procedure readily indicates the factor to which a variable makes its strongest contribution.

TABLE 4.1
(CONT.)

ROTATED FACTOR LOADINGS—1964 SURVEY ITEMS

Factor

Variable	VII	VIII	IX	X	h^2
1	−.01939	−.09887	.77893	.07231	.67174
2	.00201	.15839	.03242	.04419	.46882
3	.21136	−.00145	−.08436	−.06215	.59803
4	.09653	.05044	−.02019	−.14056	.53360
5	−.00034	−.12388	.20651	−.00007	.48199
6	.07488	.03397	−.01696	.08391	.45932
7	−.02458	.08922	−.07359	−.06200	.54294
8	.01889	.15109	−.12799	.00532	.53580
9	.08332	−.11128	.07367	−.00233	.62364
10	−.01946	.02073	−.01626	.18710	.54820
11	.01707	.20317	−.10636	−.36186	.49874
12	.02366	.10139	−.04335	.00453	.90204
13	.19353	.00590	−.01350	−.15738	.62274
14	.21830	.01502	−.01439	−.09236	.56074
15	.07360	.04461	.05439	.03484	.64181
16	.05000	.08113	.05593	−.08494	.62135
17	.00513	.00392	−.01317	.06281	.55042
18	.03138	.08554	−.00815	−.08260	.44938
19	.30854	.23739	−.12964	.10865	.30621
20	.24972	.12508	−.05095	−.00811	.35503
21	.10042	−.00054	.06836	−.25690	.42546
22	.08638	.28586	−.02949	−.03039	.44920
23	.00098	−.03706	−.04018	−.79217	.66939
24	−.00953	.67442	−.04270	.04796	.54648
25	.25155	.62055	.06428	−.07249	.50324
26	.67023	−.03414	−.03017	.00385	.49799
27	.63495	.04697	−.02951	.12602	.44795
28	.03402	−.25861	−.52843	.04231	.64041
29	.00511	−.16179	−.46820	.07694	.62643
30	−.01771	.06732	.11396	.09118	.41132
31	.36508	.19574	,10891	−.04978	.37883
32	.34575	.21678	.11268	−.30448	.40870
33	.60950	.09716	.01370	−.17059	.43672
34	.04684	−.03621	.15242	.02114	.48218
35	.11536	.20232	−.00548	.15412	.41704
Latent Root	1.49214	1.39820	1.29938	1.15447	
Cumulative % of Latents Roots	.39976	.43971	.47684	.50982	

Taken as a whole, one must conclude that this dimension represents a "long-run participation value" factor, since it measures the perceived value of elections and electoral apparatus *per se*.

FACTOR 5—PARTY CONTROL

Factor 5 reflects a desire for the control of government to change hands. However, this yearning for party competition is partly a reflection of frustrated Republicanism, as indicated by a moderate loading for Republican Party identification (item 29). This latent Republican insecurity may also account for the fact that the level of the regularity in voting in previous elections is also moderately correlated with this factor.

FACTOR 6—PRO-DEMOCRATIC POLICY: SOCIAL WELFARE

Federal government guaranties of jobs, a high standard of living, and medical care, and an active central government measure a dimension which can best be labeled a "social welfare" factor. The substantive direction of the factor is pro-Democratic because of the positive loadings of items 20, 21, and 22.

FACTOR 7—PRO-DEMOCRATIC POLICY: CIVIL RIGHTS

The reader will recall that attitudes on public policy were coded in a manner which expressed the perceived congruence between the respondent and a political party. The highest score indicated a perceived congruence with the Democratic Party, while the lowest score expressed a perceived consistency with the Republican Party on a given policy. The seventh factor is given substance by the civil rights questions of equal employment opportunities, school integration, and public accommodations. Since the factor loadings for these items are positive, the direction of perceived congruence is toward the Democratic Party. Consequently, this logically becomes a "pro-Democratic civil rights" factor.

FACTOR 8—PRO-DEMOCRATIC POLICY: FOREIGN AFFAIRS

Factor 9 is best defined by items 24 and 25, which relate to foreign aid and discussions with communist nations, respec-

tively. The dimension is pro-Democratic because variables 24
and 25 have high *positive* loadings.

FACTOR 9—PERCEIVED CLOSENESS

This dimension is clearly a "perceived one-sidedness" factor,
since the first item is so strongly correlated with this factor.
This dimension could be thought of as the Downsian "perceived closeness" of the election factor in reverse. It is interesting to ,note that Republican identification, as reflected by
items 28 and 29, is *negatively* correlated with "perceived one-
sidedness."

FACTOR 10—PRO-REPUBLICAN POLICY: SCHOOL PRAYERS

Variable 23 provides all that is needed for a substantive interpretation of factor 10. This dimension relates to a perceived
congruence between an individual and a party on the question
of school prayers. It is a pro-Republican dimension, since the
school prayer has a high *negative* loading.

Downsian Parameter Estimates

The preceding factor analysis provides a basis for the construction of crude indices which measure the magnitudes of the various Downsian parameters. The following scales are formed by
combining selected variables:

1. Differential Intensity Index. The intensity of the party
differential, the degree of concern over the election outcome,
and a general attentiveness constitute this scale.

2. Information Cost Index. This scale is simply the Total
Mass Media Index. This particular item loaded at .92 on the
"information cost" factor. Therefore, it is the best measure of
information costs.

3. Perceived Closeness Index. This measure is based upon
the question relating to the respondent's perception of the
closeness of the election.

4. Long-Run Participation Value Index. This index is
made up of the three survey items which reflect the value of
elections and electoral apparatus.

5. *Ideological Congruence Index.* This measure comprises the items reflecting a perceived congruence between the respondent and the political party. The reader will recall that the Simulmatics models of the 1964 presidential election used the ideological positions of voters on civil rights, nuclear responsibility, and social welfare. As inferred from the factor analysis, it is possible to construct an ideological congruence index using civil rights and social welfare attitudes. The foreign affairs factor would not really tap attitudes on nuclear responsibility. Therefore, the civil rights and social welfare items become the basic elements of this index. Constructing the scale in this manner may assist in relating the present simulation effort to previous research, especially the Simulmatics project. This index will be employed in the ideological modification of the Downsian model.

6. *Performance Rating.* The preceding factor analysis does not contain a dimension reflecting performance ratings. Therefore, the simulations will measure performance ratings by searching the list of responses to the open-ended questions on the perceptions of political parties. If responses relating to the Democratic and/or Republican party's ability or inability to manage government are present, then a performance rating can be determined in accordance with the partisan direction of the response(s). As outlined in Chapter Five, the voter with a zero party differential will utilize a performance rating only when he believes the parties have the same policies. If he perceives different policy positions, his zero party differential is a result of his expectation that his utility income will be the same regardless of which party is in power. To determine whether or not the person with a zero party differential perceives the parties as having similar policies, the same set of response vectors for the open-ended questions [5] on party perceptions are searched to see

---

[5] For this purpose, searching lists of open-ended responses seemed superior to the use of forced choice responses, since the respondent, if he so desired, could point to policy positions which he particularly liked or disliked about either party. This would be more in line with Downsian logic, since calculations of differential utility flow are individually defined. This assumes that the respondent can more readily indicate which policy differences are *personally* relevant.

if this potential voter perceives any partisan differences on a policy or set of policies he might consider relevant to his utility income. If he perceives no differences, he alters the basis of his decision to a performance rating.

Having undertaken the rather sophisticated technique of factor analysis, the obvious question arises as to why we did not use standardized factor scores as the measure of the various dimensions. An equally obvious answer is that standardized factor scores have a mean of zero and a variance of one. As a result, all scores lower than the mean value will be negative. Arbitrarily assigning zero to the mean implies that a *person with a score less than or equal to the average value for the population will have a score of zero or less.* Therefore, regardless of the nature of the election, all parameter estimates will be expressed relative to the mean value. For simulation purposes, this writer has no desire to attach a zero to the average value of an index. Therefore, each index is computed so that a resulting value ranges between 0.0 and 1.0. This is accomplished by dividing the actual score by the maximum possible score for a given index.

This attempt at measuring the parameters of the Downsian model is, at best, awkward, and at worst primitive. However, until survey questions are constructed on the basis of the Downsian model, this may be the only way to proceed with a simulation of voting behavior based upon that model.

In spite of possible measurement problems, however, we have been able to construct indices of Downsian model parameters. Consequently, each person has a score on all the relevant aspects of Downsian voting logic. The computer simulations presented in the next chapter make use of these indices to process each person through the Downsian model of voter decision-making which was outlined and flow-diagramed in Chapter Three.

5 Downsian model simulation results

In the earlier discussion of simulation as a research methodology, we stated that a model of a dynamic process could be represented in a flow chart. However, in order to ensure precise expression of the relationships embedded in the overall model, one might seriously consider translating the logic of the flow chart into a computer program. The program then becomes the model, which can be tested with data from "real-world" situations. The utility of the model is evaluated on the basis of its predictive ability. Models demonstrating high predictive power are retained, while those yielding poor predictions are rejected. Obviously two or more models with widely divergent logical relationships could predict equally well. In this instance, one would temporarily accept both models until one or both could be demonstrated to lack theoretical merit. Models, of course, cannot indefinitely be accepted as the "truth." The researcher must accept alternative explanations until he is able to reject a given model on the basis of simulation predictions.

To test the predictability of the Downsian rational actor model, the flow chart of the revised Downsian model presented in Chapter Three was incorporated in a computer program written in Fortran IV. This program, which makes use of the indices developed for estimating parameters of the model, is designed to run on an IBM 360-Model 50. The model has been

tested on a total of 1352 survey respondents included in the
University of Michigan Survey Research Center 1964 presidential election study. Results of these simulation runs are reported
below.

Original Downsian Model

The summary statistics for the Downsian simulation presented
in Table 5.1 forecast a substantial victory for Lyndon B. Johnson. One striking feature is the high level of predicted abstention. Of the total number of the respondents in the model, over
45 per cent were predicted to abstain. The effect on the aggregate predictions was to depress both the expected vote for
Johnson and for Goldwater. The overall predictive accuracy of
this model is 42.3 per cent—i.e. of those predicted to vote
Democratic, Republican, or to abstain, 42.3 per cent were correct predictions. Stated another way, 57.7 per cent were inac-
curately predicted. The reader might reasonably demand better
performance from this simulation model.

TABLE 5.1

SUMMARY STATISTICS FOR ORIGINAL MODEL,
ALL PARAMETERS AT FULL AND EQUAL WEIGHT

Votes	Number	Per Cent
Democratic		
Predicted	586	43.3
Actual	723	53.4
Abstain		
Predicted	610	45.2
Actual	282	20.9
Republican		
Predicted	156	11.5
Actual	347	25.7
Total		
Predicted	1352	100.0
Actual	1352	100.0

Per Cent Correctly Predicted = 42.3

The flow chart of the original Downsian model outlined a number of alternative paths to the final decision. Examination of the results taking place in the various branches of the model will provide insight into the strengths and weaknesses of the present simulation.

Table 5.2 is a summary of the activity occurring within the *non-zero* party differential branches of the model. The data indicate that 340, or 25.1 per cent of all respondents, calculated pro-Democratic party differentials. Of this group, 237, or 17.5 per cent of all respondents, were predicted to vote Democratic. This forecast is quite accurate, in that over three-quarters of those predicted to vote Democratic actually did cast a vote for Johnson. On the other hand, quick examination indicates that of 103 people predicted to abstain, almost three-quarters actually gave their support to LBJ. This suggests where some of the weakness lies in the model, which clearly allows for excessive non-voting. This is somewhat the case for the Republicans, as indicated by the lower portion of the table. Although only 2 per cent of the total sample are predicted to abstain, even within this small group over 60 per cent vote for Goldwater. It is interesting to note that only 6.5 per cent of the total number of respondents display pro-Republican party differentials, and a mere 61, or 4.5 per cent, are predicted to vote for the Republican candidate. The accuracy of this prediction, however, is borne out by the fact that fully 85 per cent of this group actually did vote for Barry Goldwater.

The tentative conclusion to be drawn from the observation of those individuals with non-zero party differentials is that there is an invalid relationship expressed between the cost and the benefit parameters of the model. In other words, cost, in relationship to benefits, is presently overstated in the model.

Nevertheless, it would be advantageous to examine the results for those with *zero* party differentials, since they account for over two-thirds of the total sample. Observation of the process as it unfolds in these branches of the model may provide additional understanding regarding its inadequacies. Careful inspection of Table 5.3, which presents the simulated and actual voting results for those with zero party differentials who perceive different policies but the same utility flow, reveals two

TABLE 5.2

ORIGINAL MODEL SIMULATION AND ACTUAL RESULTS FOR
THOSE WITH NON-ZERO PARTY DIFFERENTIALS

Pro-Democratic:
Predicted To Vote Democratic = 237
Per Cent of Total = 17.5

Actual Vote:		*Per Cent*
Democratic =	178	75.1
Abstain =	49	20.7
Republican =	10	4.2
Total =	237	100.0

Predicted To Abstain = 103
Per Cent of Total = 7.6

Actual Vote:		*Per Cent*
Democratic =	77	74.7
Abstain =	21	20.4
Republican =	5	4.9
Total =	103	100.0

Pro-Republican:
Predicted To Vote Republican = 61
Per Cent of Total = 4.5

Actual Vote:		*Per Cent*
Democratic =	4	6.6
Abstain =	5	8.2
Republican =	52	85.2
Total =	61	100.0

Predicted To Abstain = 27
Per Cent of Total = 2.0

Actual Vote:		*Per Cent*
Democratic =	3	11.1
Abstain =	7	25.9
Republican =	17	63.0
Total =	27	100.0

TABLE 5.3

ORIGINAL MODEL

SIMULATION AND ACTUAL RESULTS FOR THOSE
WITH ZERO PARTY DIFFERENTIALS
(PERCEIVE DIFFERENT POLICIES, SAME UTILITY)

Predicted To Randomly Vote Democratic = 82

Per Cent of Total = 6.1

Actual Vote:		Per Cent
Democratic =	43	52.5
Abstain =	12	14.6
Republican =	27	32.9
Total =	82	100.0

Predicted To Randomly Vote Republican = 78

Per Cent of Total = 5.8

Actual Vote:		Per Cent
Democratic =	42	53.9
Abstain =	16	20.5
Republican =	20	25.6
Total =	78	100.0

Predicted To Abstain = 184

Per Cent of Total = 13.6

Actual Vote:		Per Cent
Democratic =	82	44.5
Abstain =	36	19.6
Republican =	66	35.9
Total =	184	100.0

interesting developments. In the first place, the percentage predicted to abstain is wildly incorrect. Of the 184 persons expected to abstain, over 80 per cent actually cast a vote for one of the two major party candidates. Secondly, it is undeniable that, for those individuals who derive utility from voting in excess of any expected costs, the process of random selection of a candidate is an erroneous basis for a decision. In this particular branch of the model, 82 were predicted to vote Democratic, and 78 were predicted to vote Republican. It is indeed curious that for both of these cases *virtually the same proportion actually threw their support to the Democratic Party.* In other words, of those randomly predicted to vote Democratic, 43 in fact did cast such a vote, while of those who were randomly predicted to vote Republican, 42 ended up on the *Johnson* bandwagon.

This review indicates that even when a citizen has a zero party differential and does not perceive a difference in utility to be derived from the parties, he does not make voting decisions randomly. Furthermore, as was the case for those with non-zero party differentials, voters were also predicted to abstain in much greater numbers than was actually the case. This failure of the random selection process to depict actual behavior is one of the more interesting findings of the present research, and will be reconsidered below.

Those respondents who perceived similar policies for both parties, and therefore displayed zero party differentials, were predicted, by and large, to either vote Democratic or to abstain (see Table 5.4). It is clear that large numbers, 19.7 per cent of the total sample, computed performance ratings which were clearly pro-Democratic. Nevertheless, the accuracy of the Democratic predictions is summarily unimpressive, since only slightly over 50 per cent actually cast a ballot for Lyndon Johnson.

Perhaps the most notable feature of this table is the fact that of the 296 who were predicted to abstain, 145 people, or 49 per cent, actually supported the Democratic candidate. Again, as has been the case in every other branch of the model, cost unduly outweighs any calculated benefits.

Sensitivity Testing

These results can be received with mixed reactions. On the one hand, a predictive accuracy of 42.3 per cent is hardly cause for celebration. On the other hand, the predictive ability of the model is not terribly disappointing in light of two important facts: (1) the survey was not designed with a Downsian frame-

TABLE 5.4

ORIGINAL MODEL

SIMULATION AND ACTUAL RESULTS FOR THOSE
WITH ZERO PARTY DIFFERENTIALS
(PERCEIVE SAME POLICIES)

Predicted To Vote Democratic = 267

Per Cent of Total = 19.7

Actual Vote:		Per Cent
Democratic	= 145	54.3
Abstain	= 75	28.1
Republican	= 47	17.6
Total	= 267	100.0

Predicted To Vote Republican = 17

Per Cent of Total = 1.3

Actual Vote:		Per Cent
Democratic	= 4	23.5
Abstain	= 2	11.8
Republican	= 11	64.7
Total	= 17	100.0

Predicted To Abstain = 296

Per Cent of Total = 21.9

Actual Vote:		Per Cent
Democratic	= 145	49.0
Abstain	= 59	19.9
Republican	= 92	31.1
Total	= 296	100.0

work in mind, and (2) the test of predictive accuracy is quite
stringent in that it calls for exact prediction and not simply a
correlation between simulation and actual results. This second
caveat requires some elaboration. Consider the earlier correlation of .70 between the Simulmatics 1960 "best fit" predictions
and actual statewide results. The .70 figure would seem to be
prima facie evidence of an altogether better model than the

Downsian simulation executed by this writer. However, the Simulmatics estimates account for only 49 per cent of the *variance* in actual election outcomes. Along the same lines, the Simulmatics 1964 five-factor model results correlated at .52 with the election returns. This means that 27.04 per cent of the *variance* of the actual electoral patterns is accounted for by the Simulmatics predictions. To offer a comparable interpretation of the Downsian computer simulation, one might state that the vote predictions accounted for 42.3 per cent of the actual election results. Considered in this perspective, the initial test of the Downsian model would appear to be generally successful.

A more profound understanding of the voter's decision-making process may be obtained by experimenting with the various parameters of the computer model. By systematically varying the relative importance of the simulation parameters, often referred to as "sensitivity testing," the researcher may be able to determine which aspects of the model add to or detract from the predictive accuracy of the computer simulation. Of course, another possible outcome is that the predictive accuracy of the model may remain unchanged under all conditions.

The method of sensitivity testing employed here is *incremental proportional weighting*. This approach involves the weighting of a given parameter by some predetermined coefficient. For example, if one were to hypothesize that information costs do not have a one-to-one relationship with the other parameters of the model, but instead have a one-to-two relationship, one would simply multiply the information cost estimate for a voter by 0.5 to get a weighted value for the parameter. If one were to hypothesize that information costs were in no way important to voter decision-making, the information cost estimate for any voter would be multiplied by zero, with the effect of dropping information costs out of the model. Conversely, multiplying a voter's information cost by 1.0 would build the parameter into the model at *full weight*. In the "experiments" reported below, the proportional weighting coefficient was initially set at 0.0. The 0.0 parameter weight was multiplied by the parameter under examination. The weight estimate was used in the model and the same kind of results presented in Tables 5.1, 5.2, 5.3, and 5.4 was produced. Then the parameter weight was *incre-*

mented to 0.1. Again, the same kind of output was obtained. The parameter weight was then *incremented* to 0.2, etc., etc. This procedure was continued until the weight was built up to 1.0, which meant that the simulation was run with all model parameters at full weight.[1] The usual results were furnished and the computer program was terminated. Since parameters were weighted proportionally and there was a systematic incrementing of the parameter weight, the author chooses to refer to this procedure as *incremental proportional weighting*.

INFORMATION COST "EXPERIMENT"

One of the consequences of the original model was the prediction of an inordinate amount of non-voting. This suggests the possibility that "information costs" were given too much emphasis in the original formulation of the Downsian model. Therefore, we hypothesized that by reducing the importance of information costs by subjecting that parameter to the incremental proportional weighting method of sensitivity testing we would get a better predictive accuracy. Furthermore, an inference could be made about the importance of information costs in the overall voter decision-making process.

Figure 5.1 is a pictorial summary of the sensitivity tests run on the Downsian model. The lines represent a plotting of each proportional parameter with the associated level of predictive accuracy.[2] A glance at the information cost line indicates that the predictive accuracy of the model is at its peak when information costs are dropped out of the model altogether (i.e. when the parameter weight is set at 0.0). In fact, by completely removing information costs from the model, the predictive accuracy of the simulation is raised to 58.6 per cent. As the impact of the information cost parameter is systematically increased from 0.0 to 1.0, the accuracy of the predictions steadily decline until only 42.3 per cent (i.e. the same level as the original model) are correctly predicted. The numerical value associated

---

[1] The simulation with all parameters at full weight is identical to the original model previously analyzed.

[2] For a summary of the predictive accuracy for each parameter weight for this and other sensitivity tests, see Appendix B.

FIGURE 5.1
SUMMARY OF PARAMETER EXPERIMENTS
ORIGINAL MODEL

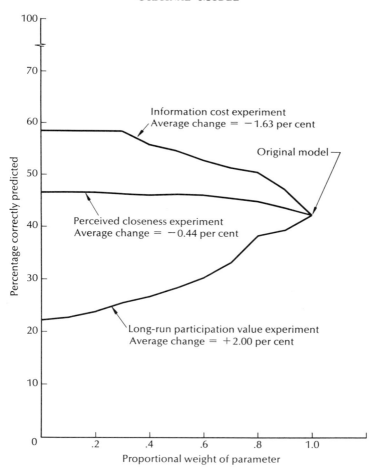

with each line represents the average change in predictive accuracy resulting from the procedure of gradually building the parameter back into the model (i.e. by incrementing parameter weight from 0.0 up through 1.0). One can see that each increment in the proportional weighting of the cost parameter brought about an average *decrease* in the predictive accuracy of the model of − 1.63 percentage points. In other words, over all ten transformations of the parameter weight, the per cent correctly predicted declined by 16.3.

One conclusion, of course, is that information costs hamper the ability of the model to predict voting outcomes, and consequently, one must entertain the possibility that information costs do not play a viable role in the rational calculus of the individual citizen. However, it is informative to probe further into the outcome of the sensitivity test of the information cost parameter.

Table 5.5 is a presentation of the summary statistics for the information cost experiment. *Results are provided for the simulation with the parameter weight set at 0.0, since the greatest predictive accuracy was achieved when information costs were completely dropped out of the model.*[3] As with the original Downsian simulation, Lyndon Johnson was predicted to gain a clearcut victory over Barry Goldwater. Three factors worth noting are reflected in the results. In the first place, Johnson's vote is undeniably overestimated. This perhaps accounts for the second interesting occurrence, which is that only a handful of voters are expected to abstain. Thirdly, the aggregate predictions for the Goldwater vote are very accurate indeed.

Table 5.6 reveals that of the 340 individuals with pro-Democratic party differentials, 331, or 24.5 per cent of the total sample, are predicted to vote Democratic. Indeed, almost 76 per cent of those predicted to vote Democratic cast a vote for LBJ. Furthermore, 86 of the 88 people with pro-Republican party differentials are predicted to vote for Goldwater. Eighty per cent of those individuals actually did cast such a vote. With information costs deleted from the decision-making model,

---

[3] For any given sensitivity test, simulation results were computed for the eleven different settings of the parameter weight. In each case, we shall report simulation outcomes only for the one parameter setting which yields the greatest departure from the overall predictive accuracy of the original model.

TABLE 5.5

SUMMARY STATISTICS FOR COST EXPERIMENT
WITH PARAMETER WEIGHT EQUAL TO 0.0

Votes	Number	Per Cent
Democratic		
Predicted	996	73.7
Actual	723	53.4
Abstain		
Predicted	37	2.7
Actual	282	20.9
Republican		
Predicted	319	23.6
Actual	347	25.7
Total		
Predicted	1352	100.0
Actual	1352	100.0

Per Cent Correctly Predicted = **58.6**

greater numbers of people with non-zero differentials are correctly predicted. It is for these citizens that the information cost
parameter is somewhat irrelevant. These are the Downsian voters who care most about who wins, which is displayed in their
clearcut party differentials. They have the least need to collect
more information since additional information is unlikely to
alter their position. Consequently, it would be unlikely that
people with non-zero party differentials would incur substantial
information costs.

Table 5.7 provides evidence that when no information costs
are incurred, the predicted level of participation almost doubles
for those whose zero party differentials are due to their per-
ceiving different policies, but the same utility. This solves the
problem of overpredicting abstention. However, the most important substantive theoretical finding is that these individuals
do not vote on a random basis when their expected benefits out-

TABLE 5.6

INFORMATION COST EXPERIMENT
SIMULATION AND ACTUAL RESULTS FOR THOSE
WITH NON-ZERO PARTY DIFFERENTIALS,
PARAMETER WEIGHT EQUAL TO 0.0

Pro-Democratic:
Predicted To Vote Democratic = 331
Per Cent of Total = 24.5

Actual Vote:		Per Cent
Democratic	= 251	75.9
Abstain	= 66	19.9
Republican	= 14	4.2
Total	= 331	100.0

Predicted To Abstain = 9
Per Cent of Total = 0.7

Actual Vote:		Per Cent
Democratic	= 4	44.4
Abstain	= 4	44.4
Republican	= 1	11.2
Total	= 9	100.0

Pro-Republican:
Predicted To Vote Republican = 86
Per Cent of Total = 6.4

Actual Vote:		Per Cent
Democratic	= 6	7.0
Abstain	= 11	12.8
Republican	= 69	80.2
Total	= 86	100.0

Predicted To Abstain = 2
Per Cent of Total = 0.1

Actual Vote:		Per Cent
Democratic	= 1	50.0
Abstain	= 1	50.0
Republican	= 0	0.0
Total	= 2	100.0

TABLE 5.7

INFORMATION COST EXPERIMENT
SIMULATION AND ACTUAL RESULTS FOR THOSE
WITH ZERO PARTY DIFFERENTIALS
(PERCEIVE DIFFERENT POLICIES, SAME UTILITY),
PARAMETER WEIGHT EQUAL TO 0.0

Predicted To Randomly Vote Democratic = 164

Per Cent of Total = 12.1

Actual Vote:		Per Cent
Democratic =	86	52.4
Abstain =	31	18.9
Republican =	47	28.7
Total =	164	100.0

Predicted To Randomly Vote Republican = 173

Per Cent of Total = 12.8

Actual Vote:		Per Cent
Democratic =	78	45.1
Abstain =	31	17.9
Republican =	64	37.0
Total =	173	100.0

Predicted To Abstain = 7

Per Cent of Total = 0.5

Actual Vote:		Per Cent
Democratic =	3	42.8
Abstain =	2	28.6
Republican =	2	28.6
Total =	7	100.0

weigh costs. Of those who are predicted to vote Democratic, 28.7 per cent voted for Goldwater. Of those who are predicted to vote Republican, 45.1 per cent lent their support to Lyndon Johnson. Indeed, the actual voting pattern displayed by respondents in this branch of the model is quite similar to the overall vote distribution for the entire sample. This suggests that the choice of a candidate is by no means a coin-tossing exercise. On the contrary, since the voting pattern resembles the distribution for the rest of the electorate, one might very well conclude that some other device, such as interaction with primary group affiliates, provides a basis for the choice of a candidate. One might reasonably expect that a voter in this branch of the model would defer to the judgment of a close associate.

Of those employing performance ratings 501, or 37.1 per cent of the total sample, voted Democratic (see Table 5.8). The predictive accuracy is slightly over 54 per cent. Here, the error is produced largely by the model's failure to forecast a sufficient amount of abstention. The accuracy of Republican predictions remained approximately the same as they were previously.

PERCEIVED CLOSENESS EXPERIMENT

Another cost factor, which could have produced excessive abstention in the original model, is the perceived closeness of the election dimension. Those who compute non-zero party differentials must discount their differential by the perceived closeness of the election. Of course, the closer the election, the less the discount rate, since the individual's vote is worth more than it would be for an expected landslide. By varying the impact of this parameter, the predictive accuracy might be improved without underestimating the level of non-voting.

Referring back to Figure 5.1, the reader will find that the predictive accuracy of the simulation model is not highly sensitive to the perceived closeness of the election factor. Indeed, the model predicts best (46.7 per cent) when the perceived closeness parameter is completely excluded from the model. However, as the parameter is incrementally built back into the model, the predictive ability of the simulation declines on an average of -0.44 percentage points per increment.

The aggregate results for this test indicate that the Democratic vote is adequately estimated (see Table 5.9). Nevertheless, too little Republican voting and too much abstention are being predicted.

The predicted voting behavior for individuals with non-zero party differentials, presented in Table 5.10, is exceedingly accurate. In fact, the behavior of approximately 74 per cent of

TABLE 5.8

INFORMATION COST EXPERIMENT
SIMULATION AND ACTUAL RESULTS FOR THOSE
WITH ZERO PARTY DIFFERENTIALS
(PERCEIVE SAME POLICIES),
PARAMETER WEIGHT EQUAL TO 0.0

Predicted To Vote Democratic = 501

Per Cent of Total = 37.1

Actual Vote:		Per Cent
Democratic	= 272	54.2
Abstain	= 123	24.6
Republican	= 106	21.2
Total	= 501	100.0

Predicted To Vote Republican = 60

Per Cent of Total = 4.4

Actual Vote:		Per Cent
Democratic	= 18	30.0
Abstain	= 6	10.0
Republican	= 36	60.0
Total	= 60	100.0

Predicted To Abstain = 19

Per Cent of Total = 1.4

Actual Vote:		Per Cent
Democratic	= 4	21.1
Abstain	= 7	36.8
Republican	= 8	42.1
Total	= 19	100.0

the 340 respondents in this branch of the model are correctly predicted. In the original model, only 61 per cent were accurately forecast. Since this parameter is not operative for other voters, outcomes for individuals with zero party differentials remain the same as they were in the original model—i.e. the results are identical to those reported in Tables 5.3 and 5.4.

TABLE 5.9

SUMMARY STATISTICS FOR PERCEIVED
CLOSENESS OF ELECTION EXPERIMENT WITH
PARAMETER WEIGHT EQUAL TO 0.0

Votes	Number	Per Cent
Democratic		
Predicted	684	50.6
Actual	723	53.4
Abstain		
Predicted	491	36.3
Actual	282	20.9
Republican		
Predicted	177	13.1
Actual	347	25.7
Total		
Predicted	1352	100.0
Actual	1352	100.0

Per Cent Correctly Predicted = 46.7

LONG-RUN PARTICIPATION VALUE EXPERIMENT

The two previous sensitivity tests demonstrated the relative impact of two parameters, which reflect types of cost. These experiments were undertaken because of the excessive abstention rate produced by the original formulation of the Downsian model. Since the elimination of both cost parameters increased the model's predictive accuracy, we hypothesized that the model would be quite sensitive to variations in the relative weight assigned to the long-run participation value, a type of benefit available to all citizens regardless of partisan loyalties. However, dropping this parameter out of the model would be expected to have the reverse effect of producing a high degree of inaccuracy. Furthermore, Downsian logic would suggest that non-voting would be almost universal.

Indeed, both expectations are borne out by the sensitivity test of the long-run participation value parameter. In the first place, only 22.3 per cent of the votes are correctly predicted. Figure

TABLE 5.10

PERCEIVED CLOSENESS OF ELECTION EXPERIMENT
SIMULATION AND ACTUAL RESULTS FOR THOSE WITH NON-ZERO
PARTY DIFFERENTIALS,
PARAMETER WEIGHT EQUAL TO 0.0

Pro-Democratic:
Predicted To Vote Democratic = 335
Per Cent of Total = 24.8

Actual Vote:		Per Cent
Democratic	= 253	75.5
Abstain	= 68	20.3
Republican	= 14	4.2
Total	= 335	100.0

Predicted To Abstain = 5
Per Cent of Total = 0.4

Actual Vote:		Per Cent
Democratic	= 2	40.0
Abstain	= 2	40.0
Republican	= 1	20.0
Total	= 5	100.0

Pro-Republican:
Predicted To Vote Republican = 82
Per Cent of Total = 6.1

Actual Vote:		Per Cent
Democratic	= 7	8.5
Abstain	= 12	14.6
Republican	= 63	76.9
Total	= 82	100.0

Predicted To Abstain = 6
Per Cent of Total = 0.4

Actual Vote:		Per Cent
Democratic	= 0	0.0
Abstain	= 0	0.0
Republican	= 6	100.0
Total	= 6	100.0

5.1 provides a clear picture of the effect of incrementally weighting the long-run participation value parameter. Gradually building this factor back into the model has the overall consequence of increasing the predictive accuracy of the model by an average of $+2.2$ percentage points per increment.

Furthermore, the aggregate statistics (Table 5.11) for this computer run (parameter weight set at 0.0) offer convincing support for the second hypothesis of high abstention rates. In

TABLE 5.11

SUMMARY STATISTICS FOR LONG-RUN
PARTICIPATION VALUE EXPERIMENT
WITH PARAMETER WEIGHT EQUAL TO 0.0

Votes	Number	Per Cent
Democratic		
Predicted	34	2.5
Actual	723	53.4
Abstain		
Predicted	1309	96.8
Actual	282	20.9
Republican		
Predicted	9	0.7
Actual	347	25.7
Total		
Predicted	1352	100.0
Actual	1352	100.0

Per Cent Correctly Predicted = 22.3

fact, 96.8 per cent of the voters do not vote when there is no expected return from voting *per se*. This is particularly noteworthy, since the 1964 presidential election was presumably a contest in which significant numbers of voters would have had fairly strong expectations concerning the parties' effect upon their utility income, even in the narrow sense of utility employed here. Nevertheless, the desire for maintaining a democracy is a source of substantial benefit to the voter and without it one can readily understand Downs's prophecy of doom.

A glance at Table 5.12 reveals that non-voting is quite fash-

TABLE 5.12

LONG-RUN PARTICIPATION VALUE EXPERIMENT
SIMULATION AND ACTUAL RESULTS FOR THOSE
WITH NON-ZERO PARTY DIFFERENTIALS,
PARAMETER WEIGHT EQUAL TO 0.0

Pro-Democratic:
Predicted To Vote Democratic = 34
Per Cent of Total = 2.5

Actual Vote:		*Per Cent*
Democratic =	23	67.7
Abstain =	10	29.4
Republican =	1	2.9
Total =	34	100.0

Predicted To Abstain = 306
Per Cent of Total = 22.6

Actual Vote:		*Per Cent*
Democratic =	232	75.8
Abstain =	60	19.6
Republican =	14	4.6
Total =	306	100.0

Pro-Republican:
Predicted To Vote Republican = 9
Per Cent of Total = 0.7

Actual Vote:		*Per Cent*
Democratic =	0	0.0
Abstain =	1	11.1
Republican =	8	88.9
Total =	9	100.0

Predicted To Abstain = 79
Per Cent of Total = 5.8

Actual Vote:		*Per Cent*
Democratic =	7	8.9
Abstain =	11	13.9
Republican =	61	77.2
Total =	79	100.0

ionable even for those with non-zero party differentials. The inaccuracy produced in this branch of the model is obvious and needs very little comment. Nevertheless, this branch of the model contains all 43 of those who were predicted to participate in the election.

Since citizens with zero party differentials are deprived of the benefits which accrue from living in a democracy, they have no reason to vote. Consequently, they all abstain. The inaccuracy of this outcome can be discerned through re-examination of Tables 5.3 and 5.4. Careful observation of these results reveals that over 75 per cent of those with zero party differentials actually voted for Johnson or Goldwater.

An unavoidable conclusion is that the long-run participation value parameter represents an essential element in the present voter decision-making model. It would appear that Downs was quite correct in underlining the importance of this factor in the voter's process of rational calculation.

Party Identification Modification

It seems appropriate to conclude tentatively that the original formulation of the Downsian model predicts fairly well. As noted, the accuracy of predictions is significantly enhanced by omitting the information cost parameter. However, the predictive accuracy of this model is not very sensitive to changes in the impact of the perceived closeness of the election parameter. Furthermore, it is unmistakable that the random basis for decision-making in the zero party differential branch (different policies, identical utility) is highly inadequate. Finally, the long-run participation value factor is critical to the predictive accuracy of the model.

In an attempt to improve the simulation's fit with real-world behavior, the original Downsian model will now be modified by incorporating the concept of party identification as a model parameter. To restate the essentials of this modified version, the decision-making process remains the same for those with non-zero party differentials. If an individual calculates an original party differential of zero, yet has a party identification which is either pro-Democratic or pro-Republican, he uses the party identification factor in lieu of the rational calculation of a party differential. If the voter's party differential and his party identification are both zero, he employs the usual decision-making process associated with zero party differentials.

The incorporation of the party identification factor produced aggregate results which were fairly accurate (see Table 5.13).

TABLE 5.13

SUMMARY STATISTICS FOR PARTY IDENTIFICATION
MODIFICATION OF ORIGINAL MODEL WITH
ALL PARAMETERS AT FULL AND EQUAL WEIGHT

Votes	Number	Per Cent
Democratic		
Predicted	664	49.1
Actual	723	53.5
Abstain		
Predicted	420	31.1
Actual	282	20.9
Republican		
Predicted	268	19.8
Actual	347	25.7
Total		
Predicted	1352	100.0
Actual	1352	100.0

Per Cent Correctly Predicted = 52.1

In fact, the predictive accuracy of the model was raised to 52.1 per cent. Lyndon Johnson was again declared the winner, and it should be noted that, on an aggregate basis at least, the Democratic vote was predicted quite accurately. As with the original model, however, the level of abstention was overestimated, lowering the level of participation for both Democrats and Republicans. Nevertheless, one might assert that since survey respondents may tend to over-report participation levels,[4] the

[4] For example, consider the fact that approximately 75 per cent of those respondents included in the simulations reported that they had

simulation results may be more accurate than the actual amount of voting reported by those who were interviewed. As one would expect, the outcomes for individuals with non-zero party differentials are identical with those presented for the original Downsian simulation.

Focusing attention on individuals with non-zero identifications (Table 5.14), it should be observed that 383, or 28.3 per cent of the sample, were predicted to cast a Democratic ballot. The accuracy of these predictions exceeds 61 per cent. The error is accounted for by overestimation of non-voting. Furthermore, of the 145 expected to abstain, 72.5 per cent actually reported voting for Lyndon Johnson. Similar results are to be found for those with pro-Republican party identifications. A group of 202, or 14.9 per cent of the sample, were expected to vote for Barry Goldwater, and over 66 per cent of these individuals actually cast such a vote. Any inaccuracy here, however, seems to be explained by the fact that 48 of these individuals predicted to vote for Goldwater claimed to have thrown their support to Lyndon Johnson. As with Democratic identifiers, those with pro-Republican partisan loyalties who were predicted to abstain reported that they voted for Barry Goldwater. Again, as the original model, the present simulation appears to overestimate the extent of non-voting.

Turning to Table 5.15, one will immediately surmise that virtually no one (twenty-five people) who has *both* zero party differentials and zero party identifications perceives differences between the parties. The majority of these people have been absorbed by the party identification parameter included in the present formulation of the Downsian model. Incorporating party identification as a salient decision-making factor has the

voted in the 1964 presidential election. This represents a much higher turnout rate than the 63 per cent of eligible voters who actually cast a vote. Of course, one might infer that the sample was not representative of the nation's voters. However, given the magnitude of the difference between the reported and actual participation rates, we tend to believe that the respondents are over-reporting turnout. Possibly, some respondents believe that non-voting represents a failure to fulfill their "citizen duty." Therefore, they would rather leave the impression that they voted, than admit they shirked their civic responsibility.

TABLE 5.14

PARTY IDENTIFICATION MODIFICATION OF ORIGINAL MODEL
SIMULATION AND ACTUAL RESULTS FOR THOSE WITH
ZERO PARTY DIFFERENTIALS AND NON-ZERO
PARTY IDENTIFICATION

Pro-Democratic:
Predicted To Vote Democratic = 383
Per Cent of Total = 28.3

Actual Vote:		*Per Cent*
Democratic	= 237	61.8
Abstain	= 109	28.5
Republican	= 37	9.7
Total	= 383	100.0

Predicted To Abstain = 145
Per Cent of Total = 10.7

Actual Vote:		*Per Cent*
Democratic	= 105	72.5
Abstain	= 25	17.2
Republican	= 15	10.3
Total	= 145	100.0

Pro-Republican:
Predicted To Vote Republican = 202
Per Cent of Total = 14.9

Actual Vote:		*Per Cent*
Democratic	= 48	23.8
Abstain	= 19	9.4
Republican	= 135	66.8
Total	= 202	100.0

Predicted To Abstain = 106
Per Cent of Total = 7.8

Actual Vote:		*Per Cent*
Democratic	= 30	28.3
Abstain	= 14	13.2
Republican	= 62	58.5
Total	= 106	100.0

attending consequence of eliminating the inadequate criterion of random selection for those who have long-run participation values outweighing information costs. Overcoming the problem created by this random selection factor may explain the increased predictive accuracy of the party identification modification of the Downsian model.

The zero party differential branch of the model, where individuals perceive similar party policies, now contains only about

TABLE 5.15

PARTY IDENTIFICATION MODIFICATION OF ORIGINAL MODEL
SIMULATION AND ACTUAL RESULTS FOR THOSE WITH
ZERO PARTY DIFFERENTIALS
(PERCEIVE DIFFERENT POLICIES, SAME UTILITY)

Predicted To Randomly Vote Democratic = 4
Per Cent of Total = 0.3

Actual Vote:		Per Cent
Democratic =	1	25.0
Abstain =	2	50.0
Republican =	1	25.0
Total =	4	100.0

Predicted To Randomly Vote Republican = 11
Per Cent of Total = 0.4

Actual Vote:		Per Cent
Democratic =	4	80.0
Abstain =	0	0.0
Republican =	1	20.0
Total =	5	100.0

Predicted To Abstain = 11
Per Cent of Total = 0.8

Actual Vote:		Per Cent
Democratic =	3	27.3
Abstain =	3	27.3
Republican =	5	45.4
Total =	11	100.0

5 per cent of the total sample (Table 5.16). This outcome is also produced by the fact that the party identification factor has siphoned off most of the individuals who previously entered this branch of the voting model.

The preceding results were produced with the party identification parameter set at full weight. Systematically varying the impact of this parameter by the method of incremental proportional weighting substantially detracts from the predictive accu-

TABLE 5.16

PARTY IDENTIFICATION MODIFICATION OF ORIGINAL MODEL
SIMULATION AND ACTUAL RESULTS FOR THOSE WITH
ZERO PARTY DIFFERENTIALS
(PERCEIVE SAME POLICIES)

Predicted To Vote Democratic = 40

Per Cent of Total = 3.0

Actual Vote:		Per Cent
Democratic	= 21	52.5
Abstain	= 18	45.0
Republican	= 1	2.5
Total	= 40	100.0

Predicted To Vote Republican = 0

Per Cent of Total = 0.0

Actual Vote:		Per Cent
Democratic	= 0	0.0
Abstain	= 0	0.0
Republican	= 0	0.0
Total	= 0	0.0

Predicted To Abstain = 28

Per Cent of Total = 2.1

Actual Vote:		Per Cent
Democratic	= 12	42.9
Abstain	= 20	35.7
Republican	= 6	21.4
Total	= 28	100.0

FIGURE 5.2
SUMMARY OF PARAMETER EXPERIMENTS
PARTY IDENTIFICATION MODIFICATION

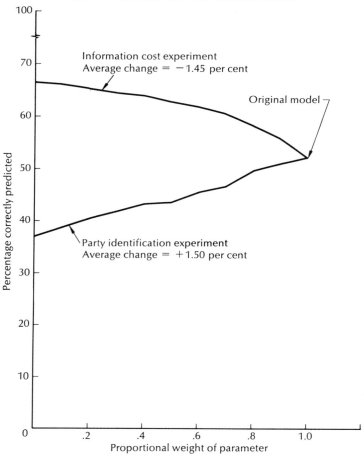

racy of the model. By completely deleting the party identification factor from the simulation model, the accuracy of the predictions are decreased by 37.1 per cent. As the party identification parameter is incrementally built back into the model, the accuracy of predicting voting outcomes increases at a rate of 1.5 percentage points per increment. This simulation result is pictorially represented in Figure 5.2. Consequently, the model demonstrates the best fit with actual electoral behavior when party identification is given maximum weight.

As with the original formulation of the Downsian model, abstention was overestimated in substantial proportions. Therefore, we hypothesized that systematic variation of the cost parameter would again demonstrate the model's sensitivity to the information cost parameter. In fact, when the information cost parameter is totally deleted from the party identification modification of the Downsian model, the actual outcomes are predicted with an accuracy of 66.6 per cent. The gradual weighting of the cost parameter has the effect of decreasing the predictive accuracy by -1.45 percentage points per increment (see Figure 5.2). Therefore, once again the model displays the best fit with real-world behavior when information costs are completely removed from the simulation.

The summary statistics for the party identification simulation with the cost parameter weight set at 0.0 indicate a clearcut victory for Johnson (Table 5.17). In this instance, however, the

TABLE 5.17

SUMMARY STATISTICS FOR PARTY IDENTIFICATION,
COST PARAMETER WEIGHT EQUAL TO 0.0

Votes	Number	Per Cent
Democratic		
Predicted	915	67.7
Actual	723	53.4
Abstain		
Predicted	38	2.8
Actual	282	20.9
Republican		
Predicted	399	29.5
Actual	347	25.7
Total		
Predicted	1352	100.0
Actual	1352	100.0

Per Cent Correctly Predicted = 66.6

forecast of aggregate Republican votes is quite accurate, while the model at the same time vastly overpredicts the electoral performance of the Democratic Party. The gross inaccuracy of the model's predictions occurs for those who claimed to have abstained. Inspection of the component branches of the model, therefore, might indicate the sources of inaccurate predictions.

In the first place, the results for individuals with non-zero party differentials are identical to those reported for the cost experiment run on the original model.

Turning to the party identification branch, note that removing information costs from the voter's rational calculus has the profound effect of virtually eliminating predictions of non-voting. In spite of the fact that Democratic and Republican votes are predicted with at least 64 per cent accuracy, it is quite evident that participation is grossly overpredicted, particularly for Democratic identifiers (Table 5.18).

As observed in the party identification modification with the cost parameter at full weight, there is no significant utilization of the zero party differential branch for individuals who perceive different policies, but identical utility flows. This again is explained by the fact that the overwhelming majority of citizens calculate either non-zero party differentials or non-zero party identifications.

Persons who perceive similar party policies are, by and large, expected to vote for Lyndon Johnson (Table 5.19). The accuracy of this prediction is 51.6 per cent. The error, in this case, is generated by overestimating the degree of participation in the election.

On a tentative basis, one is prompted to conclude that the party identification experiment produces a considerable improvement over the original model insofar as voting predictions are concerned. Furthermore, by removing the cost parameter from the model, the simulation displays a very high degree of predictive accuracy. However, this modification simultaneously causes the model to be inordinately inept at anticipating the behavior of non-voters.

TABLE 5.18

PARTY IDENTIFICATION MODIFICATION—COST "EXPERIMENT"
SIMULATION AND ACTUAL RESULTS FOR THOSE WITH
NON-ZERO PARTY IDENTIFICATIONS

Pro-Democratic:
Predicted To Vote Democratic = 513
Per Cent of Total = 37.9

Actual Vote:		*Per Cent*
Democratic	= 333	65.0
Abstain	= 129	25.1
Republican	= 51	9.9
Total	= 513	100.0

Predicted To Abstain = 15
Per Cent of Total = 1.1

Actual Vote:		*Per Cent*
Democratic	= 9	60.0
Abstain	= 5	33.3
Republican	= 1	6.7
Total	= 15	100.0

Pro-Republican:
Predicted To Vote Republican = 300
Per Cent of Total = 22.2

Actual Vote:		*Per Cent*
Democratic	= 77	25.7
Abstain	= 31	10.3
Republican	= 192	64.0
Total	= 300	100.0

Predicted To Abstain = 8
Per Cent of Total = 0.6

Actual Vote:		*Per Cent*
Democratic	= 1	12.5
Abstain	= 2	25.0
Republican	= 5	62.5
Total	= 8	100.0

TABLE 5.19

PARTY IDENTIFICATION MODIFICATION—COST "EXPERIMENT"
SIMULATION AND ACTUAL RESULTS FOR THOSE WITH
ZERO PARTY DIFFERENTIALS
(PERCEIVE SAME POLICIES)

Predicted To Vote Democratic = 62

Per Cent of Total = 4.6

Actual Vote:		Per Cent
Democratic	= 32	51.6
Abstain	= 25	40.3
Republican	= 5	8.1
Total	= 62	100.0

Predicted To Vote Republican = 3

Per Cent of Total = 0.2

Actual Vote:		Per Cent
Democratic	= 1	33.3
Abstain	= 1	33.3
Republican	= 1	33.3
Total	= 3	100.0

Predicted To Abstain = 3

Per Cent of Total = 0.2

Actual Vote:		Per Cent
Democratic	= 0	0.0
Abstain	= 2	66.7
Republican	= 1	33.3
Total	= 3	100.0

Ideological Modification

Another variation on the Downsian theme involves the voter's utilization of an "ideological differential" in lieu of a party differential. In order to incorporate an ideological differential in the model, the same procedure can be followed as that used in the party identification modification. If individuals initially computed a zero party differential, they would then attempt to differentiate the parties on the basis of ideological considerations. If such a calculation resulted in a non-zero value, the ideological differential would be used in place of the party differential. If both the party and the ideological differentials were zero, then the voter would employ one of the two zero party differential branches of the model. As indicated earlier, the ideological differential comprises items relating to civil rights and social welfare attitudes. For each individual, an average value of these items yields a simple index of ideological differentiation. This index has a range of -1.0 (pro-Republican) to $+1.0$ (pro-Democratic).

Setting the ideological differential parameter at full weight and rerunning the computer simulation produces an expected landslide for Lyndon Johnson. Needless to say, the aggregate results demonstrate that this outcome is not an appropriate description of the 1964 presidential contest (Table 5.20). Indeed, not only are the Johnson votes overpredicted, but the Goldwa-

TABLE 5.20

SUMMARY STATISTICS FOR IDEOLOGICAL MODIFICATION
WITH ALL PARAMETERS AT FULL WEIGHT

Votes	Number	Per Cent
Democratic		
Predicted	903	66.8
Actual	723	53.4
Abstain		
Predicted	388	28.7
Actual	282	20.9
Republican		
Predicted	61	4.5
Actual	347	25.7
Total		
Predicted	1352	100.0
Actual	1352	100.0

Per Cent Correctly Predicted = 47.3

ter voters become practically an extinct breed. The overall predictive accuracy of this simulation is 47.3 per cent, which is not very much better than the original Downsian simulation result (42.3 per cent).

Again, as was the case for other simulation modifications, the results for individuals with non-zero party differentials are the same as those for the original Downsian model.

Table 5.21 is a presentation of the results for individuals with non-zero ideological differentials. Of those 918 respondents, 663 are predicted to vote for Johnson, while the remainder are expected to abstain. Slightly less than half of the Democratic predictions are correct. The largest error component here is that group of people whose ideological positions are congruent with the Democratic Party, but whose vote was cast for Barry Goldwater. However, a large proportion, 21.6 per cent, of the expected Democratic support was composed of non-voters. Even greater error has been introduced for predicted abstainers, since 52.9 per cent of those respondents actually voted for Johnson. Therefore, there are, on the one hand, excessive predictions of non-voting, while, on the other hand, large numbers of predicted Democratic voters actually failed to participate in the 1964 contest.

A glance at the rest of the table underlines the fact that no one in this branch of the model demonstrates a pro-Republican ideological differential. The net result is that most of the Republican voters actually maintain ideological positions which are, on the balance, perceived to be congruent with the Democratic Party.[5] In fact, the only individuals who might have pro-Republican ideological differentials are those with non-zero party differentials. However, this group of respondents has already calculated non-zero party differentials, thereby making it unnecessary to compute an ideological differential. Furthermore, under this modification, only six people ended up in ei-

[5] This is a finding which is not inconsistent with the findings of McCloskey *et al.* See Herbert McCloskey, Paul J. Hoffman, and Rosemary O'Hara, "Issue Conflict and Consensus Among Party Leaders and Followers," *The American Political Science Review,* Vol. 54, No. 2 (June 1960), pp. 406–27.

TABLE 5.21

IDEOLOGICAL MODIFICATION,
SIMULATION AND ACTUAL RESULTS FOR THOSE WITH
NON-ZERO IDEOLOGICAL DIFFERENTIALS

Pro-Democratic:
Predicted To Vote Democratic = 663
Per Cent of Total = 49.0

Actual Vote:		*Per Cent*
Democratic	= 324	48.9
Abstain	= 143	21.6
Republican	= 196	29.5
Total	= 663	100.0

Predicted To Abstain = 255
Per Cent of Total = 18.9

Actual Vote:		*Per Cent*
Democratic	= 135	52.9
Abstain	= 53	20.8
Republican	= 67	26.3
Total	= 255	100.0

Pro-Republican:
Predicted To Vote Republican = 0
Per Cent of Total = 0.0

Actual Vote:		*Per Cent*
Democratic	= 0	0.0
Abstain	= 0	0.0
Republican	= 0	0.0
Total	= 0	0.0

Predicted To Abstain = 0
Per Cent of Total = 0.0

Actual Vote:		*Per Cent*
Democratic	= 0	0.0
Abstain	= 0	0.0
Republican	= 0	0.0
Total	= 0	0.0

ther of the zero party differential branches of the model. Since these citizens either voted Democratic or abstained, we can draw the inference that none of them could have calculated pro-Republican ideological differentials.

One can only conclude that two of the factors that seemed to work reasonably well in the Simulmatics voting model for the 1964 presidential election provide a very poor basis for correctly differentiating between Democratic and Republican voters. We hasten to add, however, that civil rights and social welfare have been given greater weight in our model. Therefore, any adverse effects these attitudes might have on simulation predictions are minimized by the Simulmatics reliance upon party identification as the basic element of the voter's decision-making process.

The zero party differential branches of the ideological modification of the Downsian model have become irrelevant, since all but six people calculate either non-zero party differentials or non-zero ideological differentials. This means that problems occurring in this branch of the model (e.g. the inappropriateness of random selection) have been eliminated. However, as the simulation predictions reported above indicate, additional problems are introduced.

Figure 5.3 illustrates the sensitivity of the present simulation to the ideological differential parameter. Completely removing this differential decreases the model's predictive accuracy to 35.3 per cent. The method of incremental proportional weighting produces an increase in the model's predictive accuracy of $+1.2$ percentage points per increment.

Running a sensitivity test on the information cost parameter produces results similar to our previous information cost experiments. The model predicts voting behavior best when the cost parameter weight is at zero. The predictions are correct 58.0 per cent of the time, and building information costs back into the model decreases the predictive accuracy of the simulation by -1.07 percentage points per parameter increment.

The aggregate voting statistics are astounding (Table 5.22), since this experiment yields an overwhelming landslide for Lyndon Johnson, who was predicted to receive 91.1 per cent of the vote. One might correctly assume that the increased predictive

FIGURE 5.3
SUMMARY OF PARAMETER EXPERIMENTS
IDEOLOGICAL MODIFICATION

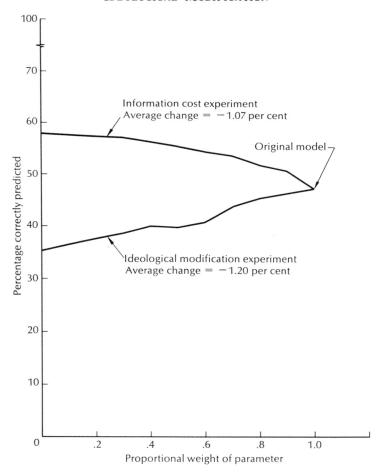

accuracy achieved in this experiment is largely a function of chance, since predicting that almost everyone will vote Democratic is bound to include just about all those who actually did cast a vote for Johnson. This computer simulation virtually creates a one-party state.

Since all predicted and actual voting patterns for those with non-zero party differentials are identical to all the other information cost experiments, we can move directly to a consideration of the ideological branch of the voting model.

TABLE 5.22

SUMMARY STATISTICS FOR IDEOLOGICAL MODIFICATION, COST PARAMETER WEIGHT EQUAL TO 0.0

Votes	Number	Per Cent
Democratic		
Actual	723	53.4
Predicted	1232	91.1
Abstain		
Actual	282	20.9
Predicted	34	2.5
Republican		
Actual	347	25.7
Predicted	86	6.4
Total		
Actual	1352	100.0
Predicted	1352	100.0

Per Cent Correctly Predicted = 58.0

For those individuals with non-zero ideological differentials, the effect of removing information costs from the model is pretty much what one might reasonably anticipate—i.e. virtually everyone is predicted to vote Democratic (Table 5.23). The 895 Democratic votes in this branch of the model alone represent 66.2 per cent of the sample. Indeed, one need go no further to discover the reason for the gross overestimation of the Johnson's electoral appeal. In spite of the fact that 50.2 per cent of these predictions are correct, one cannot overlook the 258 Republican voters who were expected to vote Democratic. There are two alternative explanations of this phenomenon: (1) the Republican voters were acting in a manner inconsistent with their own best interests, and were, therefore, manifestly ir-

TABLE 5.23

IDEOLOGICAL MODIFICATION—COST "EXPERIMENT"
SIMULATION AND ACTUAL RESULTS FOR THOSE WITH
NON-ZERO IDEOLOGICAL DIFFERENTIALS

Pro-Democratic:
Predicted To Vote Democratic = 895
Per Cent of Total = 66.2

Actual Vote:		*Per Cent*
Democratic	= 449	50.2
Abstain	= 188	21.0
Republican	= 258	28.8
Total	= 895	100.0

Predicted To Abstain = 23
Per Cent of Total = 1.7

Actual Vote:		*Per Cent*
Democratic	= 10	43.5
Abstain	= 8	34.8
Republican	= 5	21.7
Total	= 23	100.0

Pro-Republican:
Predicted To Vote Republican = 0
Per Cent of Total = 0.0

Actual Vote:		*Per Cent*
Democratic	= 0	0.0
Abstain	= 0	0.0
Republican	= 0	0.0
Total	= 0	0.0

Predicted To Abstain = 0
Per Cent of Total = 0.0

Actual Vote:		*Per Cent*
Democratic	= 0	0.0
Abstain	= 0	0.0
Republican	= 0	0.0
Total	= 0	0.0

rational; (2) these particular ideological factors were not salient features to voters in the 1964 presidential election. Because of the reasonable degree of accuracy produced by other simulations, we prefer the latter interpretation, which would consign civil rights and social welfare issues to a more peripheral role for the 1964 contest.

6 SRC six-component simulation results

We will now report the simulation results for the SRC six-component voting model. Essentially the same procedure employed for the test of the Downsian model was used here. First, simulation results for the SRC model with all parameters set at full weight will be presented. Aggregate outcomes, as well as the voting patterns for the Democratic, Republican, and abstention branches of the model, will be discussed.

Furthermore, each component of the model is subjected to the incremental proportional weighting method of sensitivity testing. The output presented for the sensitivity tests will be for the parameter coefficient that yields results which deviate the most from the predictive accuracy produced by the original SRC six-component model with all parameters assigned full weight.

The results of these computer simulations will allow the author to infer which model components had the greatest salience for voter decision-making in the 1964 presidential election. Such empirical findings may also help explain the outcome of the Johnson-Goldwater contest.

Original SRC Six-Component Model

The summary statistics for the original SRC model indicate a substantial margin of victory for Lyndon Johnson (Table 6.1).

TABLE 6.1

SRC SIX-COMPONENT MODEL,
SIMULATION AND ACTUAL RESULTS

	Democratic	Abstain	Republican	Total
Actual Results				
Number	750	288	361	1399
Per Cent	53.6	20.6	25.8	100.0
SRC Original Model				
Number	888	111	400	1399
Per Cent	63.5	7.9	28.6	100.0
Component 1 Experiment				
Number	790	234	375	1399
Per Cent	56.5	16.7	26.8	100.0
Component 2 Experiment				
Number	864	170	365	1399
Per Cent	61.7	12.2	26.1	100.0
Component 3 Experiment				
Number	825	181	393	1399
Per Cent	59.0	12.9	28.1	100.0
Component 4 Experiment				
Number	856	180	363	1399
Per Cent	61.2	12.9	25.9	100.0
Component 5 Experiment				
Number	874	156	369	1399
Per Cent	62.4	11.2	26.4	100.0
Component 6 Experiment				
Number	909	156	369	1399
Per Cent	64.9	11.2	23.9	100.0

However, the Democratic vote share is significantly overestimated, while the aggregate prediction of Goldwater's electoral performance is reasonably accurate. Special attention should be paid to the estimate of non-voting, since the actual level of abstention was more than two and one-half times greater than the model forecast. This observation initially suggests a possible difficulty of the SRC model. That is to say, the SRC simulation might not offer an adequate mechanism for the accurate prediction of non-voting. However, unlike the original Downsian model, the SRC computer simulation drastically *underestimates* the extent of abstention.

A more detailed presentation of the simulation outcome is provided in Table 6.2. Observe that the predictive accuracy of the model is 69.5 per cent, which is better than any one of the

TABLE 6.2

ORIGINAL SRC SIX-COMPONENT MODEL,
SIMULATION AND ACTUAL RESULTS

Predicted To Vote Democratic = 888

Per Cent of Total = 63.5

Actual Vote:		*Per Cent*
Democratic	= 648	73.0
Abstain	= 183	20.6
Republican	= 57	6.4
Total	= 888	100.0

Predicted To Vote Republican = 400

Per Cent of Total = 28.6

Actual Vote:		*Per Cent*
Democratic	= 54	13.5
Abstain	= 63	15.7
Republican	= 283	70.8
Total	= 400	100.0

Predicted To Abstain = 111

Per Cent of Total = 7.9

Actual Vote:		*Per Cent*
Democratic	= 48	43.3
Abstain	= 42	37.8
Republican	= 21	18.9
Total	= 111	100.0

Per Cent Correctly Predicted = 69.5

Downsian model predictions. Of those expected to vote for Johnson, 73.0 per cent actually did cast a Democratic ballot. In spite of the good fit, 20.6 per cent of the 888 predicted to vote for the incumbent president were non-voters. Thus, it appears that problems of determining which individuals are non-participants occur in both the Democratic and the abstention branches of the model.

A similar outcome holds for the Republican branch of the model, in that, even though the Goldwater vote prediction is quite accurate (70.8 per cent), there is a significant amount of non-voting.

Turning to the non-voting branch of the model, the most outstanding feature is that over 60 per cent of those expected to abstain actually voted. Continued reappearance of this phenomenon would lead to infer that the model is not really capable of forecasting abstention. In fact, one could temporarily conclude that a decision to abstain may not be linked to a calculation of candidate preference.

DEMOCRATIC CANDIDATE PERCEPTION EXPERIMENT

The first sensitivity test to be run on the SRC voting model involves the Democratic Party candidate perceptions component. It was hypothesized that the predictive accuracy of the computer simulation would be highly sensitive to transformations of the weight of this parameter. Furthermore, looking back on the 1964 election, one might expect that Johnson's predicted performance would be materially affected by diminishing the relative importance of this parameter. Utilizing the method of incremental proportional weighting, vote predictions were made for each of the eleven parameter weights. Under the column labeled "Component 1" in Table 6.3, the predictive accuracy of the simulation is reported for each parameter weight employed in the sensitivity test on the Johnson perceptions parameter experiment. Cursory inspection of these levels of predictive accuracy indicates that the simulation is virtually insensitive to systematic alterations in the impact of the "Johnson" parameter. In fact, even when this parameter is removed from the simulation, the predictive accuracy of the model is 66.6 per cent.

TABLE 6.3

PER CENT CORRECTLY PREDICTED BY PARAMETER
FOR EACH OF THE SRC SIX COMPONENTS

Per Cent Correct

Parameter Weight	Component 1 Johnson Perceptions	Component 2 Goldwater Perceptions	Component 3 Group-Related Perceptions
0.0	66.6	67.0	66.9
0.1	69.5	68.8	68.9
0.2	69.5	68.8	68.9
0.3	69.6	68.9	69.0
0.4	69.8	69.0	69.2
0.5	69.8	68.9	69.2
0.6	70.0	69.0	69.3
0.7	69.8	69.2	69.4
0.8	69.8	69.3	69.4
0.9	69.8	69.3	69.5
1.0	69.5	69.5	69.5

Per Cent Correct

Parameter Weight	Component 4 Domestic Issues Perceptions	Component 5 Foreign Policy Perceptions	Component 6 Government Management Perceptions
0.0	67.9	68.4	67.9
0.1	68.9	68.9	69.2
0.2	68.9	68.9	69.2
0.3	69.0	68.9	69.3
0.4	69.1	68.9	69.4
0.5	69.2	68.9	69.4
0.6	69.4	69.0	69.2
0.7	69.5	69.1	69.2
0.8	69.5	69.1	69.3
0.9	69.5	69.1	69.3
1.0	69.5	69.5	69.5

Turning back to Table 6.1, one finds the summary statistics for this sensitivity test.[1] In the first place, removing the Democratic candidate perceptions component from the model does lower Johnson's vote total. However, the decline in LBJ's electoral strength is only marginal since he still was expected to garner 790 votes, or 56.5 per cent of all respondents.

Goldwater's total vote was not drastically altered. However, the accuracy of the aggregate prediction is impressive.

The aggregate prediction of non-voting is as accurate as it will get, even though abstention is still significantly underestimated.

Inspection of both the Democratic and Republican branches of the model (Table 6.4) should demonstrate that the predictions of Johnson and Goldwater votes were over 70 per cent accurate. However, substantial proportions of these voters, especially in the Democratic branch of the model, failed to participate in the election.

The woeful inaccuracy in predicting abstention is the most disappointing aspect of this computer run. Almost half of those expected not to vote actually voted for Lyndon Johnson. Furthermore, over 80 per cent of those citizens predicted to abstain, in reality participated in the election. In fact, fewer numbers abstained in this branch of the model than in the Democratic branch. Indeed, dropping the Democratic candidate perceptions parameter out of the model has aggravated the problem of anticipating non-voting.

REPUBLICAN CANDIDATE PERCEPTIONS EXPERIMENT

For this particular component, it was hypothesized that predictions would be sensitive to variations in the parameter weight. One might anticipate that Goldwater's performance would be

---

[1] The results reported for this experiment are for the simulation run with the parameter weight at 0.0, since the predictive accuracy deviates the most from the original model when this component is dropped out of the simulation. Examination of Table 6.3 reveals that the predictive accuracy of all sensitivity tests deviates the most from the original model when a given parameter's weight is 0.0. Therefore, subsequent reporting of simulation outcomes will be for that sensitivity test which drops a given component completely out of the model.

TABLE 6.4

SRC SIX-COMPONENT MODEL
DEMOCRATIC CANDIDATE PERCEPTIONS "EXPERIMENT,"
SIMULATION AND ACTUAL RESULTS,
PARAMETER WEIGHT EQUAL TO 0.0

Predicted To Vote Democratic = 790

Per Cent of Total = 56.5

Actual Vote:		*Per Cent*
Democratic	= 583	73.8
Abstain	= 161	20.4
Republican	= 46	5.8
Total	= 790	100.0

Predicted To Vote Republican = 375

Per Cent of Total = 26.8

Actual Vote:		*Per Cent*
Democratic	= 51	13.6
Abstain	= 51	13.6
Republican	= 273	72.8
Total	= 375	100.0

Predicted To Abstain = 234

Per Cent of Total = 16.7

Actual Vote:		*Per Cent*
Democratic	= 116	49.6
Abstain	= 76	32.5
Republican	= 42	17.9
Total	= 234	100.0

Per Cent Correctly Predicted = 66.6

seriously hampered. However, if there were a substantial degree of negative evaluation of Barry Goldwater, deleting this component from the model could work against Johnson's bid to stay in office.

This hypothesis must be rejected out of hand. Referring back to Table 6.3, the reader can easily detect the model's predictive accuracy is *less* variant under changes in the impact of the Goldwater perceptions component. Using the method of incremental proportional weighting, the range of predictive accuracy over all parameter coefficients is between 67.0 per cent and 69.5 per cent.

The summary statistics for this component indicate that neither the Democratic nor the Republican vote-getting capacity is materially affected (Table 6.1). As was true for previous simulations, non-voting was notably underpredicted.

Focusing attention upon the three constituent branches of the model (Table 6.5), one can observe that predictions of Democratic and Republican voting exceed 70 per cent accuracy. However, when both branches are combined, there is a total of 237 individuals who abstain. This represents more than four and one-half times the number of people who actually abstained in the non-voting branch of the model. In fact, an even 70 per cent of those expected to abstain actually cast a Democratic or Republican ballot. The inability to accurately determine non-voting is still present in the model when the Republican candidate parameter is effectively removed from the simulation.

GROUP-RELATED PERCEPTIONS EXPERIMENT

For this experiment it is hypothesized that the simulation predictions will be sensitive to the group-related response perceptions component, especially insofar as the Democratic Party is concerned. Nevertheless, Table 6.3 indicates that the predictive accuracy of the model is almost invariant for changes in the impact assigned to the group-related perceptions component. The greatest deviation from the predictive accuracy of the original formulation of the SRC model (69.5 per cent) occurs when the group-related response dimension is completely removed from the computer simulation. In this case, 66.9 per cent of the predictions are correct.

On a very marginal basis, the aggregate Democratic vote prediction has declined (Table 6.1). The expected Republican vote is almost identical to that of the original SRC model. There is a repeat performance with respect to non-voting—i.e. abstention is underestimated.

TABLE 6.5

SRC SIX-COMPONENT MODEL
REPUBLICAN CANDIDATE PERCEPTIONS "EXPERIMENT,"
SIMULATION AND ACTUAL RESULTS,
PARAMETER WEIGHT EQUAL TO 0.0

Predicted To Vote Democratic = 864

Per Cent of Total = 61.7

Actual Vote:		Per Cent
Democratic	= 623	72.1
Abstain	= 183	21.2
Republican	= 58	6.7
Total	= 864	100.0

Predicted To Vote Republican = 365

Per Cent of Total = 26.1

Actual Vote:		Per Cent
Democratic	= 48	13.2
Abstain	= 54	14.8
Republican	= 263	72.0
Total	= 365	100.0

Predicted To Abstain = 170

Per Cent of Total = 12.2

Actual Vote:		Per Cent
Democratic	= 79	46.5
Abstain	= 51	30.0
Republican	= 40	23.5
Total	= 170	100.0

Per Cent Correctly Predicted = 67.0

As has been the case right along, the Democratic predictions are quite accurate, but there are also large numbers of individuals who fail to vote even though the simulation designates them as Democratic supporters (Table 6.6).

Republican vote predictions attain 69.9 per cent accuracy.

TABLE 6.6

SRC SIX-COMPONENT MODEL
GROUP-RELATED RESPONSE "EXPERIMENT,"
SIMULATED AND ACTUAL RESULTS,
PARAMETER WEIGHT EQUAL TO 0.0

Predicted To Vote Democratic = 825

Per Cent of Total = 59.0

Actual Vote:		*Per Cent*
Democratic	= 605	73.4
Abstain	= 172	20.8
Republican	= 48	5.8
Total	= 825	100.0

Predicted To Vote Republican = 393

Per Cent of Total = 28.1

Actual Vote:		*Per Cent*
Democratic	= 58	14.8
Abstain	= 60	15.3
Republican	= 275	69.9
Total	= 393	100.0

Predicted To Abstain = 181

Per Cent of Total = 12.9

Actual Vote:		*Per Cent*
Democratic	= 87	48.1
Abstain	= 56	30.9
Republican	= 38	21.0
Total	= 181	100.0

Per Cent Correctly Predicted = 66.9

However, the abstention branch of the model remains highly inadequate, since almost 70 per cent of those predicted to abstain did, in fact, participate in the election.

DOMESTIC ISSUES PERCEPTIONS EXPERIMENT

Based upon the results of the Downsian ideological modification, one might logically expect that diminishing the effect of the domestic issues parameter would significantly depress Democratic voting, at least to the extent to which civil rights and social welfare issues played a role in people's thinking. In addition, the writer, with considerable hesitation, hypothesizes that the predictive accuracy of the model will be sensitive to changes in the domestic issues perceptions component.

However, Table 6.3 again demonstrates that the predictive accuracy of the simulation is virtually insensitive to systematic transformations in the weight of the domestic issues perceptions parameter.

The summary statistics for this sensitivity test (Table 6.1) display almost the same pattern of voting produced by the original SRC six-component model. Furthermore, the problem of underestimating abstention also exists for this formulation of the model.

The same problems occur with respect to non-voting: (1) too many who were predicted to vote actually abstained, and (2) the great majority of those expected to abstain actually cast a vote (Table 6.7). This error appears to be a recurring phenomenon.

FOREIGN POLICY PERCEPTIONS EXPERIMENT

For the sake of continuity, the author hypothesized that the SRC model's predictions would be sensitive to the foreign policy perceptions component. To maintain consistency with more journalistic interpretations, one would predict that removing this parameter from the simulation would be detrimental to the Democratic Party, since Barry Goldwater acquired the image of a trigger-happy warrior.

However, we again did not have the insight to realize that the model's predictions would be insensitive to changes in the foreign policy perceptions component. The greatest deviation from the original simulation's predictive accuracy occurred when the parameter weight was set at 0.0. The predictions were 68.4 per cent accurate, or only 1.1 percentage points below the 69.5 per cent accuracy of the original SRC model (Table 6.3).

The summary statistics indicate that, for all practical purposes, the aggregate Democratic vote remains unchanged (Table 6.1). For that matter, the degree of Goldwater support is not much different from the results of the original model. The

TABLE 6.7

SRC SIX-COMPONENT MODEL
DOMESTIC ISSUES PERCEPTIONS "EXPERIMENT,"
SIMULATED AND ACTUAL RESULTS,
PARAMETER WEIGHT EQUAL TO 0.0

Predicted To Vote Democratic = 856

Per Cent of Total = 61.2

Actual Vote:		Per Cent
Democratic	= 622	72.6
Abstain	= 170	19.9
Republican	= 64	7.5
Total	= 856	100.0

Predicted To Vote Republican = 363

Per Cent of Total = 25.9

Actual Vote:		Per Cent
Democratic	= 47	12.9
Abstain	= 53	14.6
Republican	= 263	72.5
Total	= 363	100.0

Predicted To Abstain = 180

Per Cent of Total = 12.9

Actual Vote:		Per Cent
Democratic	= 81	45.0
Abstain	= 65	36.1
Republican	= 34	18.9
Total	= 180	100.0

Per Cent Correctly Predicted = 67.9

greatest net effect is to produce more non-voting than was true for the SRC simulation with all parameters assigned full weight.

Examination of Table 6.8 reveals that the previous pattern of general accuracy of Democratic and Republican vote predictions also holds for this sensitivity test. However, the level of abstention in the pro-Republican and pro-Democratic branches of the model is again quite sizable. Furthermore, this formulation of the SRC model also suffers from the same ailment diagnosed for the other computer simulations—i.e. the overwhelm-

TABLE 6.8

SRC SIX-COMPONENT MODEL
FOREIGN POLICY PERCEPTIONS "EXPERIMENT,"
SIMULATION AND ACTUAL RESULTS,
PARAMETER WEIGHT EQUAL TO 0.0

Predicted To Vote Democratic = 874

Per Cent of Total = 62.4

Actual Vote:		Per Cent
Democratic	= 640	73.2
Abstain	= 180	20.6
Republican	= 54	6.2
Total	= 874	100.0

Predicted To Vote Republican = 369

Per Cent of Total = 26.4

Actual Vote:		Per Cent
Democratic	= 48	13.0
Abstain	= 56	15.2
Republican	= 265	71.8
Total	= 369	100.0

Predicted To Abstain = 156

Per Cent of Total = 11.2

Actual Vote:		Per Cent
Democratic	= 62	39.8
Abstain	= 52	33.3
Republican	= 42	26.9
Total	= 156	100.0

Per Cent Correctly Predicted = 68.4

ing majority of respondents predicted to abstain did, in reality, vote for either Johnson or Goldwater.

GOVERNMENT MANAGEMENT PERCEPTIONS EXPERIMENT

For the final sensitivity test of the SRC model, we hypothesized that changes in the government management perceptions component would produce significant alterations in the ultimate voting pattern. On the basis of the analysis by Donald Stokes,[2] one would expect that diminution of this parameter would affect the Democratic side of the ledger, since the Democrats appeared to hold an advantage for this attitude.

The computer simulation results of the present research would lead to a rejection of these hypotheses. In the first place, the predictive accuracy of the model is relatively insensitive to changes in the parameter weight. The greatest departure from the predictive accuracy of the original model occurs when the component is deleted from the simulation (Table 6.3).

Secondly, removing the government management perceptions component actually *increased* Democratic voting strength. In this simulation, Johnson received 909 votes, which was better than his performance in any other test of the simulation, including the original formulation of the model (Table 6.1). Conversely, Goldwater garnered his lowest vote total when the parameter coefficient of this component was initially set at 0.0. In spite of Stokes's findings, this factor, at least on a marginal basis, enhances *Goldwater's,* not Johnson's, chances in the election.

This divergent finding probably reflects the fact that we took into account the attitudinal position of each respondent on this component rather than employing regression analysis, which would allow one to infer the importance of a component when the scores are expressed relative to the mean value over all individuals. In this case, if a person's raw score on the dimension

---

[2] See Donald E. Stokes, "Some Dynamic Elements of Contests for the Presidency," pp. 19–28. Actually, Stokes draws the inference that in 1964 the Democrats held an edge on all components of the SRC model. His evaluations are based upon an analysis of coefficients analogous to beta weights.

were equal to the sample mean value, his standardized score would be zero. However, to test the model through computer simulation, we utilized the respondent's actual, rather than his standardized, component score. Using standard scores would obviously have been inappropriate, since a given component might be important for everyone, and not just for those whose scores departed significantly from the mean value for all respondents. At any rate, when the simulation model was applied to each individual, *one at a time,* the result was that the government management perceptions component was slightly more helpful to Goldwater, and not Johnson.

In addition, as has been the case for all previous simulations, aggregate predictions of non-voting were notably poor, since abstention was underestimated.

Table 6.9 reveals the same pattern found for all other tests of this model. Individual predictions of Democratic and Republican voting were highly accurate. However, large numbers expected to vote actually abstained, while the great majority of those predicted to abstain did, in reality, participate in the election.

The Problem of Conceptual Clarity

In general, computer simulations of the SRC six-component voting model demonstrate a high degree of predictive accuracy, both on an aggregate basis and for the Democratic and Republican branches of the model. Nevertheless, abstention does not appear to be rooted in the preferential decision-making process, a finding which also seems to hold for the Downsian model.

In spite of its predictive accuracy, the model is not sensitive to variations in any one parameter, which suggests that there is a conceptual overlapping of the model's components. In other words, if the simulation parameters are statistically interrelated, then all six components might simply reflect the same underlying phenomenon. In terms of the SRC model, this difficulty might arise when one expresses attitudes about Lyndon Johnson. Even though responses may be articulated with reference to Johnson, such perceptions may, in reality, represent the degree to which the individual has positive or negative attitudes

TABLE 6.9

SRC SIX-COMPONENT MODEL
GOVERNMENT MANAGEMENT PERCEPTIONS "EXPERIMENT,"
SIMULATION AND ACTUAL RESULTS,
PARAMETER WEIGHT EQUAL TO 0.0

Predicted To Vote Democratic = 909

Per Cent of Total = 64.9

Actual Vote:		Per Cent
Democratic	= 652	71.7
Abstain	= 186	20.5
Republican	= 71	7.8
Total	= 909	100.0

Predicted To Vote Republican = 334

Per Cent of Total = 23.9

Actual Vote:		Per Cent
Democratic	= 34	10.2
Abstain	= 52	15.6
Republican	= 248	74.2
Total	= 334	100.0

Predicted To Abstain = 156

Per Cent of Total = 11.2

Actual Vote:		Per Cent
Democratic	= 64	41.0
Abstain	= 50	32.1
Republican	= 42	26.9
Total	= 156	100.0

Per Cent Correctly Predicted = 67.9

about the Democratic Party. In this instance, the components would measure the same thing—i.e. a general partisan attachment factor. Of course, this logic could apply to the other components of the SRC model as well.

In order to discern the dimensions underlying the simulation parameters, a principal components factor analysis was applied to the SRC six-component scores.[3] The results of this statistical operation are presented in Table 6.10. Only one factor was extracted, since all remaining eigenvalues of the correlation matrix were less than 1.0, which is the customary level of acceptance. The single factor accounts for 36.8 per cent of the total variance in the dependency structure. For present purposes, it is most important for the reader to note that all components correlate with this factor at a level greater than .54.[4] Since all the components load on this single factor, one must conclude that these variables reflect one basic dimension of attitude. This

TABLE 6.10

UNROTATED FACTOR LOADINGS
FOR SRC SIX-COMPONENT SCORES—
1964 PRESIDENTIAL ELECTION

	Factor 1
Democratic Candidate Perceptions	.65762
Republican Candidate Perceptions	.59416
Group-Related Response Perceptions	.54553
Domestic Issues Perceptions	.62896
Foreign Policy Perceptions	.54656
Government Management Perceptions	.65734
Characteristic Root	2.20952
Per Cent of Variance	36.8

factor could be labeled a "Democratic Party loyalty" dimension, owing to the fact that all loadings are positive. Since the six components measure one fundamental dimension of attitude for the 1964 presidential election, this writer adopts the position that to employ a regression analysis, is somewhat misleading, since each of the components reflects a more general dimension of attitude than its name would imply. Consequently,

[3] All positive scores represented pro-Democratic orientations, while negative scores were pro-Republican. A score of zero denoted a neutral position on a given component.

[4] These are unrotated factor loadings, since a rotation cannot be performed on one factor.

in spite of the SRC six-component simulation's predictive accuracy, the overall model lacks conceptual clarity, at least for the 1964 election.

In conclusion, Table 6.11 presents a simple percentage distribution of respondents with pro-Democratic, pro-Republican, and neutral positions on each of the SRC model components.

TABLE 6.11

DISTRIBUTION OF RESPONDENTS BY PARTISAN
DIRECTION ON EACH COMPONENT (IN PER CENT)

Partisan Direction of Respondent

Component	Pro- Democratic	Neutral	Pro- Republican	Total
1	47.7	32.9	19.4	100.0
2	32.4	47.3	20.3	100.0
3	40.6	53.0	6.4	100.0
4	39.2	41.6	19.2	100.0
5	21.9	64.5	13.6	100.0
6	13.3	63.0	23.7	100.0

N = 1399

On the first five components, the Democrats enjoy an advantage over the Republicans, with the greatest plurality occurring on the group-related perceptions component (40.6 per cent to 6.4 per cent). However, the Republicans hold an edge on the government management perceptions component, at least as far as numerical strength is concerned. Therefore, since the Republicans give a better showing on this component, it is understandable that removing the government management perceptions parameter from the simulation assists *Lyndon Johnson,* and not Barry Goldwater.

7 A revised process model of voting behavior

The purpose of this final chapter is to suggest an alternative theoretical formulation of the voting process. The basic assumptions of the revised model will be stated and amplified, where possible, by drawing upon the major empirical findings of the present computer simulations. From these fundamental assumptions, the author will deduce a set of relationships which depicts the process of voter decision-making. Finally, both the assumptions and hypothesized relationships will be integrated in such a manner as to produce a complete theoretical model of individual voting behavior.

Assumptions

1. The non-centrality of politics. The most basic assumption to be made is that politics does not occupy a position of central importance in the lives of most Americans. Quite to the contrary, social and economic factors embedded in one's relationships with family, friends, and work associates represent the primary motivating forces in the lives of the overwhelming majority of citizens.

Despite the frequent high degree of economic and social significance of many political acts, politics is not of prime importance. Even when political events are most salient (e.g. at election time or during occasional sporadic events such as riots and demonstrations), it is not long before they are displaced by the more important social and economic concerns of everyday life.

2. Political socialization provides the individual with a partisan attachment. The simulations performed here emphasize the importance of party identification as a relevant parameter in voting behavior. In the first place, the Downsian model was undeniably improved by incorporating party identification. Secondly, the SRC model components degenerated to univariate space when it was demonstrated that all six parameters actually reflected a more general dimension of partisan loyalty. In spite of the conceptual difficulties of the six SRC components, one can only conclude that party identification is a primary determinant of voting behavior, since the SRC simulations predicted election outcomes with a high degree of accuracy.

It is presently assumed, however, that the individual learns a partisan attachment prior to attaining voting eligibility. This partisan loyalty is not necessarily related to a rational calculus performed by the "child," since political socialization research generally indicates that affect precedes cognition with respect to the internalization of a party identification.

This does not, therefore, lead to the conclusion that partisan attachment does not have a "rational" basis. Rather it is assumed that there is a "rational" foundation for party identification, since the socializing agency would not transmit a partisan loyalty which was considered to be inconsistent with its basic economic and social concerns, which are basic to everyday life.

3. Utility flow is a central element in the decision-making process. If political socialization were the single determinant of voting behavior, the political system would be stabilized to the point that significant short-range as well as long-term shifts in partisan loyalty would be pre-empted as plausible occurrences.

Therefore, it is assumed that a party differential, of the Downsian variety, is computed by every individual in each election. It is the expectation of differential utility flow that provides a basis for substantial marginal vote fluctuations, and which accounts for occasional minority party victories. Furthermore, it is change in the individual's perceptions of which party will do the most to enhance his utility income, which leads to revolutionary alterations in voting patterns. For example, it should be self-evident that the last major realignment of the electorate, which occurred in the 1930s, was prompted by social and economic conditions fundamental to everyday life. Political pundits may explain the political events of the New Deal era in ideological terms. However, the vast changes in the perceptions of which party would provide greater utility income actually provide the most tenable explanation of that particular voter revolution. The persistence of the New Deal coalition is insufficiently explained by voter calculations based on ideology. Instead, it is enough to state that the previous rational calculations of utility flow have not been successfully controverted on a sustained basis by the Republican Party.

The Downsian simulations provide some basis for this argument insofar as ideological considerations of civil rights and social welfare are concerned. *These factors could only be important for those citizens whose utility income is affected by perceived party policy on civil rights and social welfare. This fact explains why the voting behavior of people with zero party differentials could not be predicted on a purely ideological basis.*

4. *Information costs are not relevant to voter decision-making.* The individual receives enough free information that he need not deduct information costs from his party differential or party identification. Any information collected relates to the fundamental social and economic concerns of life. If this information is politically relevant, he employs it in his rational computations. The sensitivity tests run on the information cost parameter of the Downsian model lend support to this assumption.

5. *Long-run participation value is a norm transmitted by political culture, and can assume a value of zero.* Unlike Downs, we assume that the long-run participation value is a norm related to political culture, and is not added to a partisan preference. Instead, the long-run participation value is a perceptual set, which initially determines the individual's predisposition toward participating in the election. Consequently, we as-

sume that a marginal group of citizens will not *perceive* any appreciable benefit from voting *per se*—i.e. their perceived long-run participation value takes on a zero score.

Downs assumes instead that everyone has a participation value greater than zero. This is perhaps ill-conceived in light of the fact that the best simulation results were produced when information costs were removed from the Downsian model. The deletion of the information costs from the party identification modification of his model led to the overprediction of participation. Therefore, it is reasonable to assume that many individuals opt out of electoral participation prior to determining a party preference.

6. *Interaction within primary groups is a key factor in voting behavior.* Given the assumption that social and economic relations are of primary importance to the individual, a related assumption would hold that the individual links his potential decision-making to those persons most intimately involved with the most basic concerns in his life.

In some instances, the individual takes advantage of primary group interaction in order to reinforce his own predispositions, while at other times, he employs interpersonal interaction in order to eliminate uncertainty and ambivalence. This is, of course, one way of securing information as well as a means of evaluating political events.[1]

7. *The probability of any one interaction occurring is a function of the individual's interest in the present election.* By McPhee's definition, the level of "interest" is directly proportional to the strength of the individual's initial partisanship value. While a general interest in the election may be highly related to the level of partisanship, there are many instances in which the potential voter is very interested in the election, but uncertain about a partisan preference.

Propositions

1. *If the individual initially calculates a zero long-run participation value, he may vote only if interaction within his pri-*

---

[1] For elaboration on the theme of primary group interaction, the reader might find it useful to review Chapter Three.

mary groups alters his original perception of the importance of participating. This proposition is derived directly from assumptions 5 and 6. If the citizen perceives no value from voting *per se,* he declines the option of voting for a partisan choice. However, since primary group interaction is assumed to be a key factor in voter decision-making, the group may stimulate him to vote.

2. *If the individual perceives a non-zero long-run participation value, and he computes a zero party differential and maintains a neutral party identification, he will be most likely to be influenced by his primary group interactions.* Based upon assumption 5, a non-zero long-run participation value would predispose a person to be generally amenable to voting in an election. However, if his party differential (assumption 3) and his party identification (assumption 2) are both neutral, he has no basis for selecting a candidate. Rather than basing his decision upon a random selection process, which was shown to be an inappropriate basis for making a choice, he enters the interaction phase of decision-making.

In this instance, the individual has no partisan orientation to promote among his associates. Consequently, he is not likely to assume the role of opinion leader.

This logic departs somewhat from the McPhee approach (see Chapter Three) since this proposition argues that interaction, in this instance, is utilized not for social validation of an initial preference, but to attain social cues which might provide a basis for deciding upon a preference. Nevertheless, interaction may produce further ambivalence, which would occasion abstention.

3. *If the individual calculates a non-zero participation value, and his party identification and party differential are incongruent (or either is zero), he is likely to be influenced during primary group interaction.* The deductive logic of this proposition is similar to that adopted in proposition 2. The incongruence of party identification and party differential creates a form of "attitudinal cross-pressure," which impedes the individual's ability to influence his peers. As a result, this potential voter is more likely to be influenced during the interaction phase of decision-making. Therefore, primary group interaction would

serve the purpose of providing cues which would enable the individual to reduce the initial cognitive dissonance generated by incongruent party identification and party differential calculations.

The effectiveness of primary group interaction in resolving this attitudinal conflict is, of course, a function of the primary group's consensus on the most preferred partisan position. That is, if the primary group very strongly favors the individual's party identification, the individual is most likely to resolve his attitudinal conflict by voting in accordance with his party identification. If the voter's party differential is heavily favored by members of his peer groups, it is most probable that his preference will be determined by the party differential factor. Ambivalence or lack of agreement within one's primary groups is likely to be manifested in a continued indecisiveness on the part of the individual, in which case he will most likely abstain.

4. If the individual computes a non-zero long-run participation value, and his party identification and party differential are congruent, he will become an opinion leader during primary group interaction. This particular citizen enters interaction with a very strong and consistent partisan orientation, since his party identification and expected utility flow are mutually reinforcing. This person, therefore, is instrumental in determining the overall partisan stance of the primary group.

Consequently, in this instance, primary group interaction provides the individual with social validation of an initial preference. In other words, it is this type of participant who is most like the individual represented in McPhee's socio-psychological model. However, the McPhee simulation assumes that disagreement between the individual and a discussion partner causes the individual to hold his decision in abeyance, pending further external stimulation. The present theory allows for direct primary group influence (especially under proposition 3) without additional external stimuli. We presently hypothesize that, even if the individual exposes himself to additional stimuli which are *external to the primary* group, his re-evaluation of political objects will be highly dependent upon partisan orientations maintained by individuals with whom he has already interacted.

As stated under proposition 4, the individual will most likely vote in accord with initial calculations. However, if he interacts with close associates, who have equally strong but counter partisan orientations, it is possible for him to experience ambivalence, in which case he would abstain. Alternatively, he may feel obliged to alter the direction of his party differential.[2] In this instance, he is likely to expose himself to additional interaction but would not assume the role of a forceful opinion leader, since he would be experiencing incongruence between the decisional components. These last two occurrences would, however, be highly infrequent.

A Revised Voting Model

Given the preceding assumptions and propositions, a tentative model of voting behavior can now be constructed in such a manner as to incorporate the relevant parameters of voter decision-making. The model that follows will *not* be a precise, operational expression of the process of voting behavior. Instead, the revised theoretical relationships will be presented in a general way in order to provide a basic outline of the voting process.

The revised model, which is based upon simulations performed at the sociological, the socio-psychological, and the individual levels of analysis, is presented in the flow chart in Figure 7.1.

The model indicates that the political culture has equipped the individual with basic orientations toward political objects in his environment. For example, the process of political socialization is the basic mechanism facilitating the individual's internalization of attitudes toward the political parties and toward being an active participant.

His general attitudinal orientations toward participating in elections are activated in a manner designed to give his long-run participation value specific reference to the election presently at hand. If the long-run participation value, when applied

---

[2] We assume that an individual's long-term party identification would not be changed by short-term influences. Change of party identification could take place in a later stage of the model.

FIGURE 7.1
REVISED VOTING PROCESS MODEL

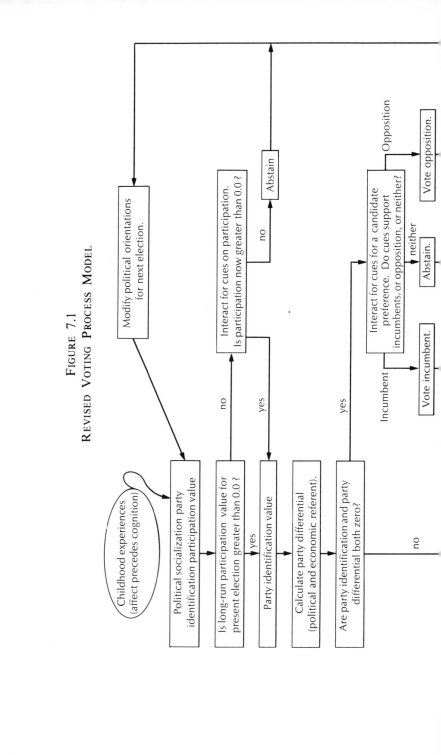

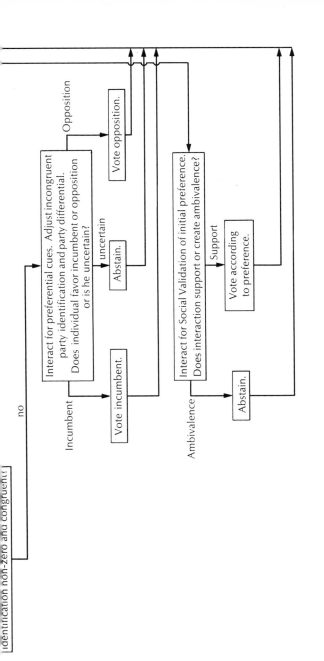

Identification non-zero and congruent?

no

Interact for preferential cues. Adjust incongruent party identification and party differential. Does individual favor incumbent or opposition or is he uncertain?

Incumbent

Opposition

uncertain

Vote incumbent.

Abstain.

Vote opposition.

Interact for Social Validation of initial preference. Does interaction support or create ambivalence?

Ambivalence

Support

Abstain.

Vote according to preference.

to the present election period, is zero, he enters the interaction phase of the model. If interaction does not alter his initial long-run participation value, the person abstains (proposition 1). Otherwise, the individual proceeds to the preferential phase of the model (proposition 1).

Individuals favorably predisposed toward voting in the election would then employ their party identification and party differential in order to determine their preference among the available candidates. If both of these factors were neutral, the citizen, who still maintains a non-zero long-run participation value, would enter the interaction stage of the model. Although Downs forecast that this voter would select a candidate at random, the present research has indicated that the selection process for this type of participant is anything but random. In fact, the actual results for this group of voters more closely resembles the rest of the electorate than an outcome produced by random choice. The mechanism proposed to rectify this weakness is primary group interaction. The individual's interpersonal relationships with his primary groups would provide social and economic cues for deciding upon a preference (proposition 2). Of course, interaction may reinforce the individual's ambivalence, in which case he would abstain. At any rate, this individual would probably be the recipient of influence attempts made by his peers (proposition 2).

Individuals who calculate strong and congruent party differentials and party identifications are those who utilize any interaction to socially validate their preference (proposition 4). Certain enough of their position that they probably could not be persuaded to vote in a manner inconsistent with their original calculations, these participants are just not "switchers." In addition, most primary group interactions would provide an opportunity for these individuals to assume the role of "opinion leaders" (proposition 4).

The flow chart indicates that people who compute incongruent party differentials and party identifications employ primary group interaction as an adjustive process, which leads to the choice originally dictated by either the party differential or the party identification. Of course, primary group influence may be inconclusive for the individual's calculations, in which case he would abstain. The individual in this branch of the model would probably *receive* influence from primary group associates (proposition 3).

To complete the voting process, the voter modifies his party identification and long-run participation value. This phase of the model allows each election to have an impact on the individual's political orientations. The continuation of the socialization process through time accounts for the stabilization of partisan attitudes for most voters, and allows for short- and long-term changes among a relatively small number of citizens.

The general outline of this revised voting model requires two important caveats. In the first place, the 1964 presidential election may be sufficiently unlike any other election that our simulations may not be generalizable to other electoral contests. Secondly, the present use of all the models discussed may be inappropriate. In other words, it may be unnecessary for this author to propose a revised model.

In spite of any such substantive and/or methodological shortcomings, we tentatively offer this revised voting model. Future tests of this and other models should provide for surveys geared to the computer simulation approach to the study of voting behavior. The present study was designed to subject deductive theoretical models to inductive empirical testing, the results of which have implications for deductive models of voting behavior. The preceding inductive analyses (i.e. the computer simulations) have provided the basis for revised voting process models—a general strategy which facilitates a much needed interaction between deductive logic and inductive testing in political analysis.

APPENDIX A
Survey Items Included in Factor Analysis

Variable 1:
(If R makes choice) "Do you think it will be a close race or will ———— win by quite a bit?"

Variable 2:
"Do you think it will make any difference in how you and your family get along financially whether the Republicans or Democrats win the election? (How is that?)" (If makes a difference and not answered) "Do you think you'll be better off or worse off financially if the Democrats win the election?"

Variable 3:
"Some people don't pay much attention to the political campaigns. How about you, would you say that you have been very much interested, somewhat interested, or not much interested in following the political campaigns so far this year?"

Variable 4:
"People like me don't have any say about what the government does."

Variable 5:
"Voting is the only way that people like me can have a say about how the government runs things."

Variable 6:
"Sometimes politics and government seem so complicated that a person like me can't really understand what's going on."

Variable 7:
"I don't think public officials care much what people like me think."

Variable 8:
"How much did you read newspaper articles about the election—regularly, often, from time to time, or just once in a great while?"

Variable 9:
"How about radio—did you listen to any speeches or discussions about the campaign on the radio?" (If yes) "How many programs about the campaign did you listen to on the radio—a good many, several, or just one or two?"

Variable 10:

"How about magazines—did you read about the campaign in any magazines?" (If yes) "How many magazine articles about the campaign would you say you read—a good many, several, or just one or two?"

Variable 11:

"How about television—did you watch any programs about the campaign on television?" (If yes) "How many television programs would you say you watched—a good many, several, or just one or two?"

Variable 12:

Mass Media Usage Index (number-based variables 8–11).

Variable 13:

"Some people don't pay too much attention to election campaigns. How about you—were you very interested in this campaign, fairly interested, just slightly interested, or not interested at all in it?"

Variable 14:

"Some people seem to think about what's going on in government all the time whether there's an election going on or not. Others aren't interested. Would you say you follow what's going on in government?"

Variable 15:

"How much do you feel that political parties help make the government pay attention to what the people think?"

Variable 16:

"And how much do you feel that having elections makes the government pay attention to what the people think?"

Variable 17:

"How much attention do you think most Congressmen pay to the people who elect them, when they decide what to do in Congress?"

Variable 18:

"Over the years, do you think that control of the government should pass from one party to the other every so often, or do you think that it's all right for one party to have control for a long time?"

Variable 19:

"Some people think the government in Washington should help towns and cities provide education for grade and high school children, others think this should be handled by the states and local communities. Have you been interested enough in this to favor one side over the other?" (If yes) "Which are you in favor of?"

        combined with

"Which party do you think is more likely to want the government to help local communities provide education for our children, the Democrats, the Republicans, or wouldn't there be any difference between them on this?"

Variable 20:

"Some people are afraid the government in Washington is getting too powerful for the good of the country and the individual person. Others feel that the government in Washington has not gotten too strong for the good of the country. Have you been interested enough in this to favor one side over the other?" (If yes) "What is your feeling?"

combined with

"Which party do you think is more likely to favor a stronger government in Washington, the Democrats, the Republicans, or wouldn't there be any difference between them on this?"

Variable 21:

"Some say the government in Washington ought to help people get doctors and hospital care at low cost, others say the government should not get into this. Have you been interested enough in this to favor one side over the other?" (If yes) "What is your position?"

combined with

"Which party do you think is more likely to want the government to help in getting doctors and medical care at low cost, the Democrats, the Republicans, or wouldn't there be any difference between them on this?"

Variable 22:

"In general, some people feel that the government in Washington should see to it that every person has a job and a good standard of living. Others think the government should just let each person get ahead on his own. Have you been interested enough in this to favor one side over the other?"

combined with

"Which party do you think is more likely to favor the government's seeing to it that each person has a job and a good standard of living, the Democrats, the Republicans, or wouldn't there be any difference between them on this?"

Variable 23:

"Some people think that it is all right for the public schools to start each day with a prayer. Others feel that religion does not belong in the public schools but should be taken care of by the family and the church. Have you been interested enough in this to favor one side over the other?"

combined with

"Which party do you think is more likely to allow the schools to start each day with a prayer, the Democrats, the Republicans, or wouldn't there be any difference between them on this?"

Variable 24:

"We now come to a few questions about our country's dealings with other countries. How about aid to foreign countries. Some say that we should give aid to other countries if they need help, while others think each country should make its own way as best it can. Have you been interested enough in this to favor one side over the other?"

combined with

"Which party do you think is more likely to give aid to other countries, the Democrats, the Republicans, or wouldn't there be any difference between them on this?"

Variable 25:

"Some people think our government should sit down and talk to the leaders of the communist countries and try to settle our differences, while others think we should refuse to have anything to do with them. Have you been interested enough in this to favor one side over the other?"

combined with

"Which party do you think is more likely to sit down and talk with the leaders of communist countries, the Democrats, the Republicans, or wouldn't there be any difference between them on this?"

Variable 26:

"Some people feel that if Negroes (colored people) are not getting fair treatment in jobs the government in Washington ought to see to it that they do. Others feel that this is not the federal government's business. Have you had enough interest in this question to favor one side over the other?"

combined with

"Which party do you think is more likely to want the government to see to it that Negroes (colored people) get fair treatment in jobs, the Democrats, the Republicans, or wouldn't there be any difference between them on this?"

Variable 27:

"Some people say that the government in Washington should see to it that white and Negro (colored) children are allowed to go to the same schools. Others claim that this is not the government's business. Have you been concerned enough about this question to favor one side over the other?"

combined with

"Which party do you think is more likely to want the government to see to it that white and Negro (colored) children go to the same schools, the Democrats, the Republicans, or wouldn't there be any difference between them on this?"

Variable 28:

"Looking ahead, do you think the problem of keeping out of war would be handled better in the next four years by the Republicans, or by the Democrats, or about the same by both?"

Variable 29:

"Generally speaking, do you usually think of yourself as a Republican, a Democrat, an Independent, or what?" (If Republican or Democratic) "Would you call yourself a strong (Republican) (Democrat) or not a very strong (Republican) (Democrat)?" (If Independent or other) "Do you think of yourself as closer to the Republican or Democratic party?"

Variable 30:

"In the elections for President since you have been old enough to vote, would you say that you have voted in all of them? Most of them? Some of them? Or none of them?"

Variable 31:

"Some people think it's all right for the government to own some power plants while others think the production of electricity should be left to private business. Have you been interested enough in this to favor one side or the other?"

combined with

"Which party do you think is more likely to want the government to own electric plants, the Democrats, the Republicans, or wouldn't there be any difference between them on this?"

Variable 32:

"Some people say that our farmers and businessmen should be able to go ahead and do business with communist countries as long as the goods are not used for military purposes. Others say that our government should not allow Americans to trade with the communist countries. Have you been interested enough in this to favor one side over the other?"

combined with

"Which party do you think is more likely to allow farmers and businessmen to trade with communist countries, the Democrats, the Republicans, or wouldn't there be any difference between them on this?"

Variable 33:

"Congress passed a bill that says that colored people (Negroes) should have the right to go to any hotel or restaurant they can afford, just like white people. Some people feel that this is something the government in Washington should support. Others feel that the government should stay out of this matter. Have you been interested enough in this to favor one side over another?"

combined with

"Which party do you think is more likely to favor the government supporting the right of colored people (Negroes) to go to any hotel or restaurant, the Democrats, the Republicans, or wouldn't there be any difference between them on this?"

Variable 34:

"Generally speaking, would you say that you personally care a good deal which party wins the presidential election this fall or that you don't care very much which party wins?"

Variable 35:

"About what do you think your total income will be this year for yourself and your immediate family?"

APPENDIX B
Summary of Results for Sensitivity Tests of Downsian Models

Per Cent Correctly Predicted

ameter eight	Cost Experiment–Original Model	Participation Experiment–Original Model	Closeness Experiment–Original Model
0.0	58.6	22.3	46.7
0.1	58.5	22.8	46.8
0.2	58.4	23.8	46.7
0.3	58.4	25.4	46.3
0.4	55.8	26.7	46.0
0.5	54.9	28.3	46.1
0.6	52.8	30.3	46.0
0.7	51.3	33.1	45.4
0.8	50.6	38.1	44.9
0.9	47.2	39.3	43.8
1.0	42.3	42.3	42.4

	Party Identification–Modification	Party Identification–Cost Experiment	Ideological Modification	Ideological Cost Experiment
0.0	37.1	66.6	35.3	58.0
0.1	38.9	66.1	36.7	57.9
0.2	40.4	65.5	37.6	57.4
0.3	41.9	64.7	38.9	57.2
0.4	43.2	64.1	40.0	56.4
0.5	43.4	63.0	39.8	55.5
0.6	45.6	62.0	41.9	54.6
0.7	46.7	60.7	43.9	53.8
0.8	49.8	58.4	45.3	51.9
0.9	51.0	56.0	46.4	50.8
1.0	52.1	52.1	47.3	47.3

BIBLIOGRAPHY

Books

Alker, Hayward R., Jr., *Mathematics & Politics,* New York: Macmillan, 1965.

Barton, Richard F., *A Primer on Simulation and Gaming,* Englewood Cliffs, N.J.: Prentice-Hall, 1970.

Bentley, Arthur F., *The Process of Government,* Chicago: University of Chicago Press, 1908.

Berelson, Bernard, Lazarsfeld, Paul F., and McPhee, William N., *Voting,* Chicago: University of Chicago Press, 1954.

Beshers, James M. (ed.), *Computer Methods in the Analysis of Large-Scale Social Systems,* Cambridge, Mass.: M.I.T. Press, 1968.

Borko, Harold (ed.), *Computer Applications in the Behavioral Sciences,* Englewood Cliffs, N.J.: Prentice-Hall, 1962.

Campbell, Angus, Converse, Philip E., Miller, Warren E., and Stokes, Donald E., *The American Voter,* New York: John Wiley, 1964.

Campbell, Angus, Gurin, Gerald, and Miller, Warren, *The Voter Decides,* Evanston, Ill.: Row, Peterson, and Co., 1954.

Cattell, Raymond Bernard, *Factor Analysis,* New York: Harper, 1952.

Cherryholmes, Cleo H., and Shapiro, Michael J., *Representatives and Roll-Calls: A Computer Simulation of Voting in the Eighty-Eighth Congress,* Indianapolis, Bobbs-Merrill, 1968.

Coplin, William D. (ed.), *Simulation in the Study of Politics,* Chicago: Markham, 1968.

Dahl, Robert A., *Who Governs?,* New Haven: Yale University Press, 1961.

Dawson, Richard, and Prewitt, Kenneth, *Political Socialization,* Boston: Little, Brown, 1969.

Downs, Anthony, *An Economic Theory of Democracy,* New York: Harper, 1957.

Easton, David, and Dennis, Jack, *Children in the Political System: Origins of Political Legitimacy,* New York: McGraw-Hill, 1969.

Edwards, Allen L., *Experimental Design in Psychological Research,* New York: Holt, Rinehart and Winston, 1960.

———, *Techniques of Attitude Scale Construction,* New York: Appleton-Century-Crofts, 1957.

Edwards, Ward, and Tversky, Amos, *Decision-Making,* Baltimore: Penguin Books, 1967.

Feigenbaum, E. A., and Feldman, J., *Computers and Thought*, New York: McGraw-Hill, 1963.

Festinger, Leon, *A Theory of Cognitive Dissonance*, Evanston, Ill.: Row, Peterson, and Co., 1957.

Flanigan, William H., *Political Behavior of the American Electorate*, Boston: Allyn and Bacon, 1968.

Fruchter, Benjamin, *Introduction to Factor Analysis*, New York: Van Nostrand, 1954.

Green, Bert F., Jr., *Digital Computers in Research*, New York: McGraw-Hill, 1963.

Greenstein, Fred I., *The American Party System and the American People*, Englewood Cliffs, N.J.: Prentice-Hall, 1963.

————, *Children and Politics*, New Haven: Yale University Press, 1965.

Guetzkow, Harold (ed.), *Simulation in Social Science: Readings*, Englewood Cliffs, N.J.: Prentice-Hall, 1962.

Guetzkow, Harold, Alger, Chadwick F., Brody, Richard A., and Snyder, Richard C., *Simulation in International Relations: Developments for Research and Teaching*, Englewood Cliffs, N.J.: Prentice-Hall, 1963.

Hays, William L., *Statistics for Psychologists*, New York: Holt, Rinehart and Winston, 1963.

Harman, Harry Horace, *Modern Factor Analysis*, Chicago: University of Chicago Press, 1960.

Hess, Robert D., and Torney, Judith V., *The Development of Political Attitudes in Children*, Chicago: Aldine, 1967.

Hoggart, Austin Curwood, and Balderston, Frederick, *Symposium on Simulation Models: Methodology and Applications to the Behavioral Sciences*, Cincinnati: South-Western Publishing Co., 1963.

Horst, Paul, *Factor Analysis of Data Matrices*, New York: Holt, Rinehart and Winston, 1965.

Hovland, Carl I., Janis, Irving L., and Kelley, Harold H., *Communication and Persuasion*, New Haven: Yale University Press, 1963.

Hyman, Herbert, *Political Socialization*, New York: The Free Press, 1959.

Janda, Kenneth, *Data Processing: Applications to Political Research*, Evanston, Ill.: Northwestern University Press, 1965.

Janis, Irving L., *et al., Personality and Persuasibility*, New Haven: Yale University Press, 1962.

Katz, Elihu, and Lazarsfeld, Paul F., *Personal Influence*, New York: The Free Press, 1955.

Kendall, M. G., *A Course in Multivariate Analysis*, London: Charles Griffin, 1965.

Kessel, John H., *The Goldwater Coalition*, Indianapolis: Bobbs-Merrill, 1968.

Key, V. O., Jr., *American State Politics: An Introduction*, New York: Alfred A. Knopf, 1966.

Key, V. O., Jr., *The Responsible Electorate*, Cambridge, Mass.: The Belknap Press of Harvard University Press, 1966.

Lane, Robert E., *Political Life: Why and How People Get Involved in Politics*, New York: The Free Press, 1959.

Lane, Robert E., and Sears, David O., *Public Opinion*, Englewood Cliffs, N.J.: Prentice-Hall, 1964.

Langton, Kenneth P., *Political Socialization*, New York: Oxford University Press, 1969.

Lasswell, Harold, *Politics: Who Gets What, When, How*, New York: The World Publishing Co., 1964.

————, *Psychopathology and Politics*, New York: The Viking Press, 1960.

Lazarsfeld, Paul F., Berelson, Bernard, and Gaudet, Hazel, *The People's Choice*, New York: Duell, Sloan and Pearce, 1944.

Loehlin, John C., *Computer Models of Personality*, New York: Random House, 1968.

McPhee, William N., *Formal Theories of Mass Behavior*, New York: The Free Press, 1963.

McPhee, William N., and Glaser, William, *Public Opinion and Congressional Elections*, New York: The Free Press, 1962.

Morrison, Donald F., *Multivariate Statistical Methods*, New York: McGraw-Hill, 1967.

Naylor, Thomas H., Balintfy, Joseph L., Burdick, Donald S., and Chu, Kong, *Computer Simulation Technique*, New York: John Wiley, 1966.

NewComb, T. N., *The Acquaintance Process*, New York: Holt, Rinehart and Winston, 1961.

Orcutt, Guy H., Greenberger, Martin, Korbel, John, and Rivlin, Alice M., *Microanalysis of Socioeconomic Systems: A Simulation Study*, New York: Harper & Row, 1961.

Polsby, Nelson W., and Wildavsky, Aaron B., *Presidential Elections*, New York: Scribner's, 1964.

Pomper, Gerald M., *Elections in America*, New York: Dodd, Mead, 1968.

Pool, Ithiel deSola, Abelson, Robert P., and Popkin, Samuel, *Candidates Issues & Strategies: A Computer Simulation of the 1960 and 1964 Presidential Elections*, Cambridge, Mass.: M.I.T. Press, 1965.

Reitman, Walter R., *Cognition and Thought*, New York: John Wiley, 1966.

Rosenberg, Milton J., et al., *Attitude Organization and Change*, New Haven: Yale University Press, 1963.

Scammon, Richard M. (ed.), *America Votes 6*, Washington, D.C.: Governmental Affairs Institute, 1966.

Seal, Hilary, *Multivariate Statistical Analysis for Biologists*, London: Spottiswood, Ballantyne & Co., 1966.

Sorauf, Frank J., *Political Parties in the American System*, Boston: Little, Brown, 1964.

Stephan, Frederick F., and McCarthy, Philip J., *Sampling Opinions,* New York: John Wiley, 1963.

Thurstone, L. L., *Multiple-Factor Analysis,* Chicago: University of Chicago Press, 1947.

Tomkins, Silvan S., and Messick, Samuel, *Computer Simulation of Personality,* New York: John Wiley, 1963.

Truman, David B., *The Governmental Process,* New York: Alfred A. Knopf, 1951.

Veldman, Donald J., *Fortran Programming for the Behavioral Sciences,* New York: Holt, Rinehart and Winston, 1967.

Verba, Sidney, *Small Groups and Political Behavior: A Study of Leadership,* Princeton: Princeton University Press, 1961.

Walker, Helen M., and Lev, Joseph, *Statistical Inference,* New York: Holt, Rinehart and Winston, 1953.

Zeigler, Harmon, *Interest Groups in American Society,* Englewood Cliffs, N.J.: Prentice-Hall, 1964.

Articles and Periodicals

Abelson, Robert P., "The Use of Surveys in Simulations," *Public Opinion Quarterly,* Vol. 26 (1962), pp. 485–86.

Abelson, Robert P., and Bernstein, Alex, "A Computer Simulation Model of Community Referendum Controversies," *Public Opinion Quarterly,* Vol. XXVII, No. 1 (Spring 1963), pp. 93–122.

Abelson, Robert P., and Rosenberg, Milton J., "Symbolic Psycho-Logic: A Model of Attitudinal Cognition," *Behavioral Science,* Vol. 3 (1958), pp. 1–13.

Bernstein, Alex, and Roberts, Michael de V., "Computer vs. Chess-Player," *Scientific American,* Vol. 198 (June 1958), pp. 96–105.

Brown, Roger, "Models of Attitude Change," in Brown, R., Galanter, E., Haas, E. H., and Mandler, George, *New Directions in Psychology,* New York: Holt, Rinehart and Winston, 1962.

Cangelosi, Vincent E., and March, James G., "An Experiment in Model Building," *Behavioral Science,* Vol. 11 (1966), pp. 71–75.

Casstevens, Thomas W., "A Theorem About Voting," *The American Political Science Review,* Vol. LXII, No. 1 (March 1968), pp. 205–7.

Chapman, Robert L., Kennedy, John C., Newell, Allen, and Biel, William C., "The Systems Research Laboratory's Air Defense Experiments," *Management Science,* Vol. 5 (1959), pp. 250–69.

Cohen, K. J., Cyert, R. M., Dill, W. R., Kuehn, A. A., Miller, M. H., Van Wormer, T. A., and Winters, P. R. "The Carnegie Tech Management Game," *The Journal of Business*, Vol. XXXIII (1960), pp. 303–21.

Converse, Philip E., Clausen, Aage R., and Miller, Warren E., "Electoral Myth and Reality: The 1964 Election," *The American Political Science Review*, Vol. 59 (June 1965), pp. 321–36.

Dowling, R. E., "Pressure Group Theory: Its Methodological Range," *American Political Science Review*, Vol. LIV, No. 4 (December 1960), pp. 944–45.

Gelernter, H. L., and Rochester, N., "Intelligent Behavior in Problem-Solving Machines," *IBM Journal of Research and Development*, Vol. 2 (1958), pp. 336–45.

Glaser, William A., "Intention and Voter Turnout," *The American Political Science Review*, Vol. 52 (1958), pp. 1030–40.

———, "Television and Turnout," *The Public Opinion Quarterly*, Vol. XXIX (Spring 1965), pp. 71–86.

Goldberg, Arthur S., "Social Determinism and Rationality as Bases of Party Identification," *The American Political Science Review*, Vol. 63 (1969), pp. 5–25.

Guetzkow, Harold, "A Use of Simulation in the Study of Inter-Nation Relations," *Behavioral Science*, Vol. 4 (1959), pp. 183–91.

Hovland, Carl I., "Computer Simulation of Thinking," *The American Psychologist*, Vol. 15 (1960), pp. 687–93.

Jennings, M. Kent, and Niemi, Richard G., "The Transmission of Political Values from Parent to Child," *The American Political Science Review*, Vol. LXII, No. 1 (March 1968), pp. 169–84.

Key, V. O., Jr., and Munger, Frank, "Social Determinism and Electoral Decision: The Case of Indiana," in Burdick, Eugene, and Brodbeck, Arthur J. (eds.), *American Voting Behavior*, Glencoe, Ill.: The Free Press, 1959, pp. 281–99.

Langton, Kenneth P., and Jennings, M. Kent, "Political Socialization and the High School Civics Curriculum in the United States," *The American Political Science Review*, Vol. LXII, No. 3 (September 1968), pp. 852–67.

Levin, Murray B., and Eden, Murray, "Political Strategy for the Alienated Voter," *Public Opinion Quarterly*, Vol. 26 (1962), pp. 47–63.

McCloskey, Herbert, Hoffman, Paul J., and O'Hara, Rosemary, "Issue Conflict and Consensus Among Party Leaders and Followers," *The American Political Science Review*, Vol. 54, No. 2 (June 1960), pp. 406–27.

McCracken, Daniel D., "The Monte Carlo Method," *Scientific American*, Vol. 192, No. 5 (1955), pp. 90–96.

McPhee, William N., "Note on a Campaign Simulator," *Public Opinion Quarterly*, Vol. XXV, No. 2 (Summer 1961), pp. 184–93.

Minsky, Marvin L., "Artificial Intelligence," *Scientific American*, Vol. 215 (September 1966), pp. 246–60.

Newell, Allen, Shaw, J. C., and Simon, Herbert, "Elements of a Theory of Human Problem Solving," *Psychological Review*, Vol. 65, No. 3 (1958), pp. 151–66.

Orcutt, Guy H., "Simulation of Economic Systems," *The American Economic Review*, Vol. L, No. 5 (1960), pp. 893–907.

Pool, Ithiel de Sola, and Abelson, Robert, "The Simulmatics Project," *The Public Opinion Quarterly*, Vol. XXV (1961), pp. 167–83.

Rich, R. P., "Simulation as an Aid in Model Building," *Operations Research*, Vol. III (1955), pp. 15–19.

Riker, William H., and Ordeshook, Peter C., "A Theory of the Calculus of Voting," *The American Political Science Review*, Vol. LXII, No. 1 (March 1968), pp. 25–42.

Shapiro, Michael J., "The House and the Federal Role: A Computer Simulation of Roll-Call Voting," *The American Political Science Review*, Vol. 62 (1968), pp. 494–517.

Snyder, Richard C., "A Decision-Making Approach to the Study of Political Phenomena," in Roland Young (ed.), *Approaches to the Study of Politics*, Evanston, Ill. Northwestern University Press, 1958, pp. 3–38.

Stokes, Donald E., "Party Loyalty and the Likelihood of Deviating Elections," *Journal of Politics*, Vol. 24 (November 1962), pp. 681–702.

Stokes, Donald E., "Some Dynamic Elements of Contests for the Presidency," *The American Political Science Review*, Vol. 60 (March 1966), pp. 19–28.

Stokes, Donald E., Campbell, Angus, and Miller, Warren E., "Components of Electoral Decision," *The American Political Science Review*, Vol. 52 (June 1958), pp. 367–87.

Wilson, James Q., and Banfield, Edward C., "Public-Regardingness as a Value Premise in Voting Behavior," *The American Political Science Review*, Vol. 58 (December 1964), pp. 876–87.

INDEX

Abelson, Robert, 6, 17, 19-20, 23-24, 26, 28-29
accidental information, 59
Alabama, 31
algorithm, 16
"Alter," 41-42
anti-Catholicism factor, 26-27
approach-approach conflict, 27
Arizona, 31
avoidance-avoidance conflict, 27

Bentley, Arthur, 6
Berelson, Bernard, 6, 20-21, 43-45
best-fit simulation (Simulmatics), 28-29, 86

California, 31
Campbell, Angus, 3-4, 20, 65-66
Catholic shift factor, 26, 29
characteristic roots, 72, 135
"child," 51-52
civil rights, 30, 76, 78, 111, 114, 118, 129, 139
civil rights simulations
   Downsian, 118, 131
   Simulmatics, 28, 30
cognitive dissonance, 142
communality, 72, 74-75
computer program, 17
computer simulation
   Downsian, 53, 64, 79, 87, 114
   general, 17, 137, 147
   Simulmatics, 19

SRC model, 53, 126, 131, 133
Converse, Philip, 3, 20
correlation, 26-27, 29-30, 67, 72, 135
costs, 58, 59-61, 82, 84-85, 96
cross pressure, 21-22, 25, 27-28, 30, 141
cross-pressure pattern, 23-24
current party differential, 55-57, 59, 61, 64-65, 70-71, 73, 78, 139, 141-43, 146

"decades," 48-49, 51-52
Democratic Advisory Council, 19
Democratic candidate perceptions experiment, 120, 122-25, 135-36
Democratic Party Loyalty factor, 135
deterministic model, 12, 14-15
differential intensity index, 77
discounted party differential, 57, 61
discussion partners, 34, 41-42, 142
discussion process, 34, 41-44
domestic issues perceptions experiment, 120, 123, 128-30, 135-36
Downs, Anthony, 8, 9, 53-58, 60, 116
Downsian voting model
   accidental information, 59

civil rights simulations, 118, 131

current party differential, 55-57, 59, 61, 64-65, 70-71, 73, 78, 139, 141-43, 146

differential intensity index, 77

discounted party differential, 57, 61

Downsian model flow diagram, 62-63

Downsian rational actor, 16, 53, 56, 59, 61, 64, 79-80

expected party differential, 54

experiments, 87, 89, 106, 108, 114

future-orienting factors, 55-57, 61-63, 68

ideological congruence index, 78, 111

ideological modification, 78, 110-17, 128

ideological modification experiment, 115

ideology differential, 65, 110-12, 114

information cost experiment, 89, 92-93, 95, 106, 108-10, 114, 116-17

information cost index, 77

information costs, 58-59, 71-73, 87-88, 90-91, 100, 107, 114, 116, 139-40

long-run participation value, 60-61, 71, 73, 76, 96, 98, 100, 104, 139-43, 146-47

long-run participation value experiment, 89, 96, 98-99

long-run participation value index, 77, 100

non-zero ideological differentials, 112-14, 116-17

non-zero party differential, 82-83, 91-95, 97, 99-100, 102, 108, 110, 112, 114, 116

non-zero party identification, 102-3, 108, 109

party identification modification, 70, 100-101, 103-10, 140

party identification modification experiment, 106

perceived closeness, 77, 96

perceived closeness experiment, 84, 94, 97

performance rating, 56-57, 61, 78-79, 85

random selection process, 61, 84-85, 91, 93-94, 100, 104, 114, 141, 146

summary statistics, 81, 90, 96, 101, 107, 111

total mass media usage index, 77

trend factor, 55-56

utility income, 53-56, 60, 70, 82, 84-85, 108, 138-39, 142

vote value, 57-58

zero party identification, 102, 86, 95, 100-105, 111, 114, 139

zero party identification, 102

"dynamic" party, 48-52

"Ego," 41

eigenvalues, 72, 135

electoral college, 24

expected party differential, 54

experiments
    Downsian model, 87, 89, 106, 108, 114
    general, 17
    McPhee model, 38, 46-47, 53
    SRC six-component model, 120, 122-34

factor analysis
    characteristic roots, 72, 135
    communality, 72, 74-75
    eigenvalues, 72, 135
    general, 71, 78-79, 135
    factor loadings, 72, 76, 135
    factor scores, 79
    latent roots, 72, 74-75
    principal components, 135
    rotated factor loadings, 72, 74-75
    varimax rotation, 72

Ferguson, Jack, 7, 33, 47-48, 51

flow diagram (chart), 11, 17, 41, 53, 61, 64, 67, 79-80, 82, 143, 146

foreign affairs, 76, 78

foreign policy perceptions experi-

foreign policy (*cont.*)
    ment,   120, 123, 129-31,
    135-36
foreign policy simulation (Simul-
    matics),   28, 30
Fortran IV,   80
future-orienting factors,   55-57,
    61-63, 68

Gaudet, Hazel,   4, 20
"G" category,   36-38
"generations,"   46, 53
Goldwater, Barry M.,   30-31, 81-
    82, 91, 93, 100, 102, 111-12,
    119-20,   122,   124-20,   129,
    132-33, 136
government management percep-
    tions experiment,   120, 123,
    132-36
Green, Bert F., Jr.,   12, 18
group-related perceptions experi-
    ment,   120, 123, 126, 128,
    135-36
Gurin, Gerald,   4, 20

heuristics,   16-17
Humphrey, Hubert H.,   46-47
Hyman, Herbert,   35

ideological congruence index,
    78, 111
ideological modification,   78,
    110-17, 128
ideological modification experi-
    ment,   115
ideology differential,   65, 110-
    12, 114
incremental proportional weighting,
    87-88, 94, 98, 105, 114, 119,
    122, 124
Independents,   30
indifference,   139-41
information cost index,   77
information costs,   58-59, 71-73,
    87-88, 90-91, 100, 104, 107,
    114, 116, 139-40
interaction,   7, 43, 49, 53, 140-
    41, 146
interest,   39-41, 45, 52, 140

Johnson, Lyndon B.,   30-32, 81-
    82, 85, 91, 93, 100-102, 107-

8, 111-12, 114-16, 119, 122,
    124-25, 132-33, 136

Kennedy, John F.,   22, 24-30,
    46-47
Key, V. O., Jr.,   4, 32, 49

Lasswell, Harold,   8
latent roots,   72, 74-75
Lazarsfeld, Paul,   6, 20-21, 43-
    45
learning process,   34, 45
long-run participation value,
    60-61, 71, 73, 76, 96, 98, 100,
    104, 139-43, 146-47
long-run participation value ex-
    periment,   89, 96, 98-99
long-run participation value index,
    77, 100

Massachusetts Institute of Technol-
    ogy,   19
McPhee, William N.,   4, 7, 9,
    20-21, 33-34, 36-40, 42-48,
    52-53, 140-42
McPhee voting model
    "Alter,"   41-42
    "child,"   51-52
    "decades,"   48-49, 51-52
    discussion partners,   34, 41-
        42, 142
    discussion process,   34, 41-44
    "dynamic" party,   48-52
    "Ego,"   41
    experiments,   38, 46-47, 53
    flow diagram,   34, 42
    "G" category,   36-38
    "generations,"   46, 53
    indifference,   139-41
    interest,   39-41, 45, 52, 140
    learning process,   34, 45
    "opposition" party,   48, 50-52
    "parent,"   51
    partisanship value,   34-36, 39,
        43-46
    political immunization,   17-
        51
    stimulation process,   33, 35,
        39-40, 42-44, 53, 142
    stimulus,   33-34, 36, 38-41,
        46-49, 51-52
    stimulus intensity table,   37-
        38

storage, 34, 42
Miller, Warren E., 3, 4, 20, 65-66
Mississippi, 31
Monte Carlo method, 15-16, 16, 18, 40
Munger, Frank, 32
Murphy, George, 31

New Deal era, 20, 48, 139
New England, 31
Nixon, Richard M., 22, 24, 26-28, 46-47
non-centrality of politics, 137
non-zero ideological differentials, 112, 116-17
non-zero party differential, 82-83, 91-95, 97, 99-100, 102, 108, 110, 112, 114, 116
non-zero party identification, 102-3, 108, 109
nuclear responsibility, 30, 78

opinion leaders, 141-42, 146
"opposition" party, 48, 50-52

"parent," 51
partisanship value, 34-36, 39, 43-46
party identification, 1, 16, 29, 30, 33-35, 64-65, 70-71, 100-102, 104, 107, 138-39, 141-42, 146-47
party identification modification, 70, 100-101, 103-10, 140
party identification modification experiment, 106
perceived closeness, 77, 96
perceived closeness experiment, 89, 94, 97
performance rating, 56-57, 61, 78-79, 85
political efficacy, 73
political immunization, 47-51
political socialization, 35, 51, 138, 143, 147
Pool, Ithiel de Sola, 6, 17, 19-20, 23-24, 26, 28-29
Popkin, Samuel, 6, 17, 19-20, 23-24, 26, 28-29
primary group, 7-8, 41, 43, 49, 53, 140-42, 146

principal components, 135
propaganda, 36
Proposition 14, 31

random numbers, 15, 37
random selection process, 61, 84-85, 91, 93-94, 100, 104, 114, 141, 146
regression analysis, 67
religion, 22-27, 29-30
Republican candidate perceptions experiment, 120, 123-24, 126-27, 135-36
revised voting model flow diagram, 144-45
Roosevelt, Franklin D., 20
Roper Public Opinion Research Center, 23
rotated factor loadings, 72, 74-75

Salinger, Pierre, 31
school prayers, 77
sensitivity testing, 17-18, 26-27, 67, 85, 87-88, 96, 114, 119, 129, 131-32, 139
Shapiro, Michael J., 12-14
Simulmatics Corporation, 19, 24, 29, 32-33, 114
Simulmatics voting models
    anti-Catholicism factor, 26-27
    best-fit simulation, 28-29, 86
    Catholic-shift factor, 26, 29
    civil rights simulation, 28, 30
    cross pressure, 21-22, 25, 27-28, 30
    cross-pressure pattern, 23-24
    Simulmatics Corporation, 19, 24, 29, 32-33, 114
    "synthetic" states, 24-26
    voter-types, 23-26
Smith, Robert B., 7, 33-34, 36, 38-39, 42, 44-45, 51
social determinism, 6, 19-20, 29, 32, 36
social welfare, 30, 76, 78, 111, 114, 118, 129, 139
SRC six-component model, 8-9, 53, 65-69, 119-36, 138

SRC six-component model (*cont.*)
Democratic candidate perceptions experiment, 120, 122-25, 135-36
domestic issues perceptions experiment, 120, 123, 128-30, 135-36
experiments, 120, 122-34
flow diagram, 68
foreign policy perceptions experiment, 120, 123, 129-31, 135-36
government management perceptions experiment, 120, 123, 132-36
group-related perceptions experiment, 120, 123, 126, 128, 135-36
Republican candidate perceptions experiment, 120, 123-24, 126-27, 135-36
summary statistics, 119-20, 124, 126, 129
stimulation process, 33, 35, 39-40, 42-44, 53, 142
stimulus, 33-34, 36, 38-41, 46-49, 51-52
stimulus intensity table, 37-38
stochastic model, 12, 14-16
Stokes, Donald E., 3, 20, 65-66, 132
storage, 34, 42

summary statistics
Downsian models, 81, 90, 96, 98, 101, 107, 111
SRC six-component model, 119-20, 124, 126, 129
Survey Research Center (University of Michigan), 65-66, 69, 80
"synthetic" states, 24-26

Texas, 31
total mass media usage index, 77
trend factor, 55-56
Truman, David, 6

utility income, 53-56, 60, 70, 82, 84-85, 108, 138-39, 142

varimax rotation, 72
vote value, 57-58
voter-types, 23-26

white backlash, 31
Willkie, Wendell, 49
Wisconsin primary, 37, 46, 53

zero party differentials, 84-86, 95, 100-105, 108, 111, 114, 139
zero party identification, 102